THE JUICE MASTER'S

Ultimate Fast Food

DISCOVER THE POWER OF RAW JUICE

Everything you ever needed to know about juice

Jason Vale

author of Slim 4 Life

thorsons

Thorsons
An Imprint of HarperCollins*Publishers*
77–85 Fulham Palace Road,
Hammersmith, London W6 8JB

The website address is:
www.thorsonselement.com

and *Thorsons* are trademarks of
HarperCollins*Publishers* Ltd

First published by Thorsons 2003
This edition published by Thorsons 2004

1 3 5 7 9 10 8 6 4 2

© Jason Vale 2003

Jason Vale asserts the moral right to be
identified as the author of this work

A catalogue record of this book is available
from the British Library

ISBN 0 00 716968 X

Printed and bound in Great Britain by
Creative Print and Design (Wales), Ebbw Vale

Contents

RECITES

1

Fast Food

 Yes indeedy, fast food is without question the key to vibrant health, a slim trim bod, clear skin, longevity, and tremendous amounts of energy. Now before you decide that I am clearly a few strawberries short of a full basket and talking complete hogwash, hear me out. I can guarantee that what I think of as *fast food* is a completely different ball game from what you're thinking of (unless you've read *Slim 4 Life* of course).

When most people hear the expression "fast food", they automatically think of things like burgers, fries, pizza, and so on. The reason for this is because *fast* in this context refers to how fast the food gets to us—and there is no question that the big fast food (and I use the word food here in its loosest possible meaning) giants have got this down to a tee. However, what most people do not realize is that the minute you *eat* stuff like burgers, fries, pizza and bread-coated chicken it ceases to be fast food—in fact it turns into what I describe as *slow* food. What do I mean? Well once it's found its way into your bloodstream it . . .

. . . *slowly* clogs up your arteries, *slowly* fills your bloodstream with poisons, *slowly* overworks every organ in your body, *slowly* drains you of life, *slowly* uses up valuable nerve energy, *slowly* seeps fat into the bloodstream, *slowly* causes your red blood cells to stick together, *slowly* starves the cells in your body to death, and . . .

Slowly Leads to Overweight

So you can understand why I don't describe this type of so-called food as fast—it is very slow food. In reality, all such foods do quickly is send blood sugar levels sky high, raise blood pressure, send the heart rate racing, speed up the aging process and put you on the fast track to disease. Yep, you guessed it—I am not a fan.

As you've probably gathered by now, when I use the expression fast food I am talking about a whole different kettle of veg from the usual meaning. I'm not talking about how fast the food gets to your mouth but how fast the body will do three very important things:

Digest it
Extract the goodness
Get rid of the waste

If it does all three quickly, then it's a Juice Master fast food—if it doesn't, it isn't. Now I understand that the chances of you thinking about these three criteria every time you eat something are about as strong as the chances of getting your nasal hairs plucked by J-Lo while holding a four-leaf clover, but you should consider them. I'd even go as far as to say it's essential, as the rewards for subjecting your diet to such simple scrutiny are truly magnificent. The cost of *not* thinking about it and simply popping any old rubbish down your esophagus can be truly horrific.

If you want mind-blowing energy levels, sparkling bright white eyes, shiny hair, hard nails, strong healthy bones, glowing skin, amazing mental and physical vibrancy, and the ability to live your one and only life in a slim, trim, energy-driven, disease-free body, then listen up, listen hard, and do yourself a massive favour by actually *reading* this book . . . yes all of it! Most people who buy a book of this nature flick through every now and then, but in order to get the *full* benefits this book has to offer please read it *all*, at least once.

NOT YA REGULAR JUICING BOOK

Now if you're scratching your head thinking "isn't this supposed to be a book about juicing", well it is—but it's much more than that, too. It not only features the kind of stuff you might expect—oodles of recipes, the A–Z of fruit and veg, what to look for when buying fruit and veg, how to prepare them for juicing, what machines to buy, and so on—but it also has plenty of information on certain foods that I would strongly advise skipping, and some *mental* inspiration—the true key to life-long juicing and supreme health.

Those of you who have read my first book, *Slim 4 Life: Freedom from the Food Trap,* will already know how passionate I am about helping people to make massive changes to their health and lifestyle and just how easy-peasy-lemon-squeezy it can be when you have a bit of knowledge and are inspired. For those who have yet to read it, do yourself a favor and get a copy—especially if you feel you are addicted to certain foods and drinks and have been struggling with diets of any kind. It will show you how to free yourself from what I call "The Food Trap". In the meantime, I want to provide as much information as I can on the Juice Master way of thinking for all the newcomers—and provide some key reminders, plus some fresh information for all the "Slim 4 Lifers".

The first thing all the newcomers need to be fully aware of (and Slim 4 Lifers reminded of) is just how important *real fast food* is to mental and physical vibrancy and a slim, trim bod—and again I don't mean burgers and fries! I'm talking here about foods that are easily digested, whose "life force" is easily extracted, whose nutrients are easily used, and whose waste is easily eliminated. I'm talking here about super-rich, super-fast, nutrient-packed, *natural* fast food. By the time you finish this book you will have a whole new idea of what fast food really means. One piece of information that is bound to stick is this . . .

it takes more nerve energy to digest junk food than it does to do virtually any other activity

Here's your first eye opener—the average person will consume over 75 tons of food in their lifetime. Not only is that a huge amount but nothing you do will ever come close to the amount of nerve energy needed to deal with such a huge mass of food. Apart from—wait for it—lovemaking! This, I'm told, takes more nerve energy than anything else you can do. It may not seem like it sometimes, but making love supposedly takes up a hell of a lot of nerve energy—a good excuse for falling asleep afterward if ever there was one. Even running a marathon requires less nerve energy than the amount needed to digest junk food. I know that sounds unbelievable; running a marathon is very tough, and if you talk to someone after they've crossed the line they are of course tired and very short of breath—but they are still awake. Try interviewing the average person after they've finished their Christmas or Thanksgiving dinner—pretty tricky when they're asleep!

Do you know why people fall asleep after a big meal? Because the body is overwhelmed by the amount of junk it is being subjected to all at once and it simply doesn't have the nerve energy to cope. After all, the body not only has to digest it, it also has to try and extract any hint of nutrients from the food, deliver them to the cells, and then muster up the energy to try and eliminate the waste. This doesn't even take into account the incredible energy and enzymes needed to turn this food into blood, muscle, and bone; or the fact that the stomach, intestines, pancreas, liver, and kidneys all have to work their socks off to help process this mound of "food". So when a large, all-sorts-of-everything meal is eaten, the body looks for every available resource of energy in order to try and break down the mass, extract whatever it can from it, get rid of whatever it can, and then store what it can't get rid of (usually in fat cells). And why do we fall asleep? What it comes down to is this . . .

the body doesn't have enough nerve energy to keep you alive and awake at the same time

How scary is that? This means that if you fall asleep after a big meal, you are effectively in a coma. The body needs all hands on deck in this emergency situation, and eyesight, hearing, and consciousness are the first to be called upon in order to conserve energy and direct it toward dealing with the nightmare amount of foodstuffs that have come into the system all at once. So while to all and sundry you seem calm and cosy in the land of Nod, there is in fact complete mayhem going on inside—it's literally red alert for all internal departments. Once the body has somehow miraculously managed to deal with the *immediate* emergency, it will provide just enough energy for you to open your eyes, turn the pages of the TV guide, and press the buttons on the remote control. You won't be brimming with energy though, because the body still needs plenty to carry out the mammoth task of processing the many courses of slow-food you have just consumed.

OK, so Christmas and Thanksgiving dinners are a once-a-year thing, but there are many, many occasions throughout the year when we drift into what I call a slow-food coma. And when we're not actually completely wiped out and in a slow-food coma, we are either suffering from the physical and mental effects of one and/or in that semicomatose state we like to call normality.

You Health Freak

Because virtually everyone in the United States eats and drinks the same kind of processed—what I call—junkie foods and drinks on a regular basis—and because most of us are leading incredibly sedentary lifestyles (otherwise known by Slim 4 Lifers as "furniture disease")—our view of what constitutes "normal" health and energy levels has become just a tad warped. We now think it's perfectly "normal" to be lethargic, overweight, and under the constant mental and physical stress that inevitably goes along with a congested system. We think it's perfectly normal to arrive at the young age of 40/50/60 with arthritis, osteoporosis, damaged livers, shattered kidneys, irritable bowel syndrome, and so on, and don't think it at all odd to wake up after six to eight hours sleep and still feel tired. At the same time, we have now reached the stage where if you look good, have energy, are fit as a fiddle and eat wholesome, nutrient-rich foods, you are seen as a freak—a "health freak" to be precise. We are the only creatures on the planet who consider it odd if one of our own kind is *not* poisoning themselves on a regular basis. In fact, we now think it's strange if someone *does* eat the food nature intended and completely bizarre if they actually exercise every day for the sheer fun of it! After all, the saying is "health freak", not what it should be—

Disease Freak

I cannot really criticize this way of thinking, as I was the first to shout "health freak" some years ago when I was tired, lethargic, asthmatic, overweight, and diseased. But why do we do this? Why do we slag off those who have decided to get fit, eat healthily, and look good? Should it really be considered "freaky" to feel energetic, to eat well, drink well, sleep well, and feel fantastic? Surely it should be normal. Nobody describes a koala bear as a freak if it eats eucalyptus leaves, do they? We don't consider it odd or freakish if a badger eats grubs and runs around a lot; nor do we find it surprising if a human puts gas in a car. Why? Because, in truth, we would think them slightly bonkers if they did anything else. I mean, how insane would it be if you saw someone deliberately putting diesel fuel into a gas-driven car? How much more ludicrous would it be if they tried to justify what they were doing by saying, "I'm doing this because you only get one life and I want to live it—I'm not one of those gasoline conformists"?

So why, oh why is it that when a human being—apparently the most intelligent species on the planet—eats and drinks junk, is constantly tired and lethargic, hardly moves their body, is a completely different shape from what nature intended, and suffers from various minor (or major) ailments, do we describe these people as "normal"?

The reason is simple—the vast majority of people in the Western world are ill. The vast majority of humans in the West are waking up every day with what I call a "junkie food hangover". The vast majority of us are walking around in this slow-food coma we regard as normality.

The problem is most of the time people don't realize it because they don't stand out—compared to *most* people they are doing OK, thank you very much. Someone who has bundles of energy, looks good, feels good, and eats well *does* stand out—so we call them a freak. And if they're drinking something as strange as carrot and spinach juice and go down to the gym most days, then we really do think they're a couple of carrots short of a full bunch . . . or do we?

Knocking Down Your Neighbor's House to Make Yours Look Better

In reality we would all *ideally* love to look good, eat well, sleep well, have amazing health, and enjoy physical and mental vibrancy. However, if we think for whatever reason it's not within our power to achieve such goals then we constantly try and justify our eating habits and lifestyles—not only to other people, but also to ourselves. We say it so loud so often even *we* end up believing it—hence sayings like, "I'm fat and I'm happy", "You could get run over by a bus tomorrow". At the same time, we try and bring the fit-looking, carrot-juice-drinking, healthy people down by claiming they're "boring, no-life, health freaks" whenever we get the chance. After all, what's easier—making the effort to improve your own home, or knocking down your neighbor's nice-looking place to improve the look of yours?

The good news is, contrary to what many people believe, it is actually spookily easy to get your own "house" in order. All you need is a dollop of the *correct* knowledge, a pinch of mental inspiration and at least a glass a day of nutrient-packed, health-promoting, disease-preventing ultimate fast food.

Talker or Walker?

I have written this book because of my firsthand experience of juicing and health. OK, so I'm probably the most passionate person in the world when it comes to "juice power", but that is because I've experienced the amazing physical and mental benefits to be had from drinking nature's finest nectar every day, and I want to share it with the world. I am not a doctor, and I don't pretend to be, but I am a scientist—not in the academic or "I have umpteen certificates coming out of my backside to say I am" sense of the word, but in a much more important *experiential* sense. I have been my own guinea pig when it comes to juicing—I even drank nothing, and I do mean *nothing*, but fruit and veg juices for three months once (don't panic, I will not be recommending this, as it's madder than Maddie the mad moose). However, the eating-drinking-way-of-thinking ultimate health plan that I recommend is very sane, very easy, and, what's more, it works. I know this for certain as I do it *every day*—I "walk my talk" as they say. And what are my qualifications for writing this book? Well what about this for a "CV" . . .

was—overweight, extremely unhealthy (severe asthma, eczema, covered from head to toe in psoriasis), lacking in energy, and eating a diet that consisted of anything . . . providing it wasn't green of course!

now—asthma-free, eczema-free, 90 per cent clear of psoriasis, and living life in a slim, energy-driven, vibrant body.

I"m not telling you this to show off, but simply to show— to show you and everyone else that no matter how many times you've *tried* in the past to have better health, a slim body, or just a better diet, it *can* easily be achieved—when you know how.

What you're holding is a very simple approach to health and vitality that works—but it will only work if you read the whole book and then "do it". So many people "talk" great health, and I know that most of you reading this book *already* know what you need to eat and drink to be slim and healthy—I mean you hardly need to be Dick Tracy to figure out that fruit and veg are good and junk food is bad now do you? However, I also know that despite virtually everyone knowing what to do, they don't actually do what they know. Most of you at this stage are "talkers" not "walkers". That's not a criticism, as advertising, brainwashing, peer pressure, and misinformation lead us to make "fuel" choices that are a far cry from what nature intended for our magnificent machines. That's the reason I couldn't write a "normal" juicing book—we need to counteract some of this misinformation so that you'll be in a mentally inspired position; one where you get to the point of actually *wanting* to do it—where you become a true walker, not a talker.

Remember, Juicing Is for Life—Not Just for New Year

The object of this book is not to get you into a hyped-up "juice fad" for a few weeks and then for you to leave your juicer on a shelf to gather dust for the next year, only to end up in your next yard sale—sound familiar? No, the object is for you to juice on a *daily* basis so that you experience its amazing effects. For that to happen I not only need to inspire you with all the information needed for a juicy and fruitful life, but I also need to free your mind of the clutter by unloading some of the "apparent" pieces of vital, complicated information that, in terms of actually making the change, . . .

2

We Don't Need to Know

 As your health is the single most important thing in the world, I want to ask you some questions to test your knowledge on this vital subject. What is a bioflavinoid? What is riboflavin? Do you know? What is a free radical? How many vitamins are there? Any ideas? How much protein do you need daily? What is the best source of vitamin C? How many phytochemicals are there in a tomato? What is a phytochemical? What does vitamin K do for you? Do you have any clue as to your BMI? What is the main use of calcium in the body? What is a calorie? If you do *not* know the answers to these questions—good! We don't need to know.

A little over one hundred years ago we didn't even know what a vitamin was, and we wouldn't have known what a bio-*what-the-hell-are-you-babbling-about*-flavinoid was if it jumped up and bit us on the bum. As for your Body Mass Index, or BMI as it's known, if you asked someone back then to calculate their height by weight to see if they were in a "healthy fat range" they would have sent you straight to the funny farm. Yet despite the fact that we hadn't a clue what on earth a vitamin or mineral was, we still got here, didn't we?

Think about it; a chimpanzee doesn't give a monkey's about how much calcium, protein, fatty acids, and phytochemicals there are in the green leaves it munches daily. And I don't imagine for a millisecond it loses sleep over its BMI, RHR (resting heart rate), or the best source of vitamin B6—do you? The reason why wild animals don't know this stuff, yet still live healthy, vibrant, slim, disease-free lives, is because *they don't need to know*.

They already have access to the best "nutritionist" in the world— instinct. And luckily for us, if we peel away the influence of years of hard-hitting advertising, conditioning, brainwashing, and misinformation we've been subjected to, we all have access to this life giver/saver known as instinct. Hence sayings such as "I know I shouldn't . . . but . . . ."

This is why you already *instinctively* know what's good and what's bad, and it's why everything I say in this book will instinctively make perfect sense to you.

Weighing up the Fat

It really shows how much we have stopped relying on our own common sense and natural instincts when we not only measure things like our BMI, but we weigh our bodies to see if we are overweight. Can we not see when we are overweight? Don't we *instinctively* know when we feel sluggish and tired and have a few extra rolls of unwanted fat, that things aren't right? Do we need a set of scales to show us? Isn't it obvious? So why do we do such things? Are we all a couple of grams short of an ounce? Or have we simply been conditioned to eat and drink certain junk foods and drinks and at the same time seek help for the effects of this from people who have complicated the whole issue of health and weight loss?

Calories Don't Mean Jack

One of the main problems is that we have seen the *majority* of people doing the same nonsensical things for so many years that we tend to just follow suit without questioning what we are doing. Take calories, for example. A calorie is the amount of energy (heat) needed to raise one gram of water by one degree centigrade. Does this knowledge make an iota of a difference to your health—no! There is not one wild animal that knows how many calories are in the food they're eating and they have no idea as to what their calorific intake should be for the day—why? Because they don't need to know.

If you are thinking that we are better off knowing such stuff, ask yourself why? We apparently know more about "good nutrition" now than ever before, yet heart disease is the number one killer disease in Western society.

We not only blind ourselves with all this apparent essential nutrition "stuff", but entire industries have been built on our fears. We spend billions on vitamin and mineral tablets every year in the United States alone. And for what? To try and counter the effects of all the processed and de-natured food we are consuming.

There are a whopping 40,000 phytochemicals in just one tomato. What is a phytochemical? It's a name for a vitamin that hasn't been formally named yet. Are there really 40,000 vitamins in one tomato? I don't know and I don't care because as long as I get it into to my body, *I don't need to know*. In truth, all we need to know is that fruits and vegetables, as a whole, contain every single vitamin, mineral, bioflavinoid and, phytonutrient that we have found a name for and a million more we haven't. The fact that fruits and veg contain elements whose purpose/role we have yet to identify is vital—it means that they have an "X factor", a part of the nutritional jigsaw that we are unaware of and cannot replicate in a pill.

The body works in unison, synergistically—meaning as a *whole*. Each department within us is part of the same company, and when an apparent "simple" apple enters the body—the *whole* company benefits and it's bonuses all round. These can take the form of brighter eyes, healthy skin, a slim trim body, hard nails, shiny hair and some nice protection against all disease. Equally, put some "junkie slow food" in and the *whole* company suffers and it's pay cuts all round. Unfortunately these types of pay cuts don't affect your pocket, but every part of your life. These can take the form of lethargy, dull eyes, brittle bones, excess fat, shortness of breath, rotting teeth, and less resistance to every disease on the planet. This is why I don't really understand things like ears, nose, and throat specialists—it's as if these areas are a completely separate arm of the company?

Blah! Blah! Blah!

So many people make the whole business of health as complicated as nuclear physics—usually by trying to completely blind us with science using what I call blah, blah, blah language. This is what names like "bioflavinoid" are all about. Don't you think it's funny that when they make amazing "new" discoveries about fruits and veg they don't call them something simple? No, they opt for words like "isothiocyanates" or "riboflavin"—well they are impressive names, aren't they? These are names that say to the world, "look at me, I've spent great wads of cash on my education and by Jove you're gonna know about it".

I want to make sure you have an "all-you-need-to-know" understanding of juicing and health so that you are inspired to do it *daily* and, as a result, begin to experience the many incredible bonuses that are to be had from getting juiced. This is why I won't be using bundles of blah, blah, blah language, or complicating the issue with particular juices for particular illnesses. In truth, all you need is a good regular intake of fresh juice to begin to counteract the ill effects of your past diet and to deal with any processed food that you will be consuming (oh come on—this is nutrition for reality here!).

In Case You *"Want"* to Know

Having said all that, because a bit of good publicity can't go wrong, and due to people simply *wanting* to know, I have, in the A–Z of fruits and veg section of this book, included some nutritional information. I want to make this point clear, though—I am including this information in case you want to know, not because you *need* to know.

But before we get started on the practical stuff, we still need the dash of *correct* knowledge and that wonderful pinch of inspiration. On the knowledge front let's have a look at . . .

3
What We *Do* Need to Know

Over the years I think just about every "food" on the planet has come in for some kind of criticism—with the notable exception of fresh fruit and veg. Although having said that, the late Mr. Atkins somehow managed to put fruit in the same category as chocolate bars. These foods nourish every cell in the body, help to prevent disease, flush the system of waste, contain more bio-what's-its than you can rattle a plum at, and there isn't a single person on the planet with any shred of common sense that could possibly argue against these magnificent foods. Instinctively we all just know these foods are right; we don't need the government to tell us that we should eat at least five portions of fruit and veg every day— we already know we should.

What we don't know is the real truth about the other "foods" on the shelves. This is where our common sense and natural instinct can easily be overridden by people who are interested not in our supreme health and longevity, but in what's in our pockets. Advertisement after advertisement, product placement after product placement, years upon years of misinformation by soooo many people—including the government, the diet industry, some doctors, our own parents and teachers—have lead to a nation with very confused, conditioned, and brainwashed minds when it comes to what the hell we should be eating. We have not only reached the stage where we believe we can "feed emotions" with junkie-like drug foods, but we now even believe that some disease-causing foods—ones that were never meant for human consumption—are actually good for us. We don't have time to go into every foodstuff on the planet or how they manipulate our minds and emotions to consume disease-promoting rubbish—that's *Slim 4 Life* territory—but because I really want you to have the juice of life, I feel it's vital to give you a very brief overview of the most important so-called foods to either reduce drastically or avoid altogether.

Are You Made of the White Stuff?

This is what I mean about misinformation and conditioning. Milk, yes good old calcium-rich cow's milk—what could be healthier? Well, if you are over the age of three, I'd say just about anything. Cow's milk and the products made from cow's milk (cheese, cream, etc.) were simply never designed to be consumed by humans. I know that many people reading this book will believe that milk is a fantastic food source, but that's only because of what we've been conditioned to believe by the dairy industry and the government for God knows how many years. If we open our minds and think about it rationally we would all soon realize that the milk of a cow was meant for a calf—*not* a human. Not convinced? Well, we are the only mammals on the planet that drink milk after weaning age—even cows don't drink milk. Milk contains a protein called casein; it also, as you will no doubt be aware, contains calcium. However, what they don't tell you is that casein and calcium are chemically bound together and in order for the protein to be used efficiently and calcium utilized properly, the body has to have a couple of digestive enzymes to split them up. "So what", you may be saying, "it's all sounding a tad blah, blah, blahish". Well here's the problem: after the age of three the majority of us no longer have the enzymes that were meant for this job (another big clue as to why we shouldn't be consuming it).

Something else they don't tell you either; the protein casein is used as a base in one of the strongest wood glues—and cow's milk has over

300 times more casein than human milk. This stuff sticks to the walls of your stomach, sticks to your intestines, and creates an extremely mucous environment for many people. It prevents any good stuff you consume from being properly absorbed and hinders the elimination of wastes. Isn't it amazing how we can all be conditioned to believe something that, when looked at rationally, doesn't make a blind bit of sense? I'm not saying don't eat cheese ever again, and I'm not part of the anti-milk police; if you want it—have it. Just don't delude yourself into believing it's a health food. Over in the U.K. we had an advertising slogan for milk that read "Are you made of the white stuff?" In fact we're not made of the right stuff to deal with the white stuff.

Much of the propaganda regarding milk has been about calcium and the danger of getting brittle bones if you don't drink the stuff. What they know, but keep a little hush, hush, is that dairy products are *not* vital for good bone health. As Dr. Tierry Brun points out, "The Chinese consume no cow's milk or dairy products, yet they have among the lowest rates of osteoporosis in the world". Another fact that seems to be kept a little quiet is that all fruit, and veg contain "usable" calcium, with dark green, leafy veg such as broccoli, spinach, and kale being particularly rich sources. But it's the humble onion that is your best bet against weak bones. A study from the University of Bern in Switzerland found that just one gram of onion a day is enough to strengthen your skeleton.

As you might have guessed, you won't find any cow's milk or yogurt in my smoothies (mind you, you won't find any onion either). You will, however, find some live organic goat's yogurt in some smoothies, for reasons I'll go into later.

Mystery Food

Here's a food group that you will do yourself a massive favor skipping —"mystery food". You may not have seen this on any government food group table, but it's out there and it's being eaten by millions of us every single day. The fast food giants are perhaps the biggest sellers of it, but you'll also find tons of it in supermarkets, movie theaters, and sports stadiums. Yes, as you may have guessed, "mystery food" is a group of foods that contain ingredients that are a complete mystery. Chicken burgers, beef burgers, chicken Kiev, chicken nuggets, sausages, and so on are all examples of mystery food. It's funny how it is the law that you have to put clear labels on foods sold in packets, yet when you buy this stuff over the counter it seems exempt from any kind of ingredients regulation. I believe they should not only have an exact list of all, and I mean *all*, the ingredients in mystery foods, but a government health warning wouldn't go amiss either.

Having said that, many of the "foods" on shelves that *do* have labels require you to have a degree in blah, blah, blah language to decipher what the hell is in them—these too are definitely classified as "mystery foods". Often people ask me what to look for on a label to see if it's a good food; my reply is often "If it's got a label . . ."—after all you don't see an ingredients label on apples do you?

100% Pure Beef

What you think you're getting is often not meat at all but a load of synthetic, man-made, chemically bound "foodstuffs"—a small percentage of which might actually be some meat. Take a hot dog, for instance— what the hell is it? Well, now that you've asked, it's simply the intestines of an animal stuffed with . . . yep, mystery food! And don't be fooled by the many fast food outlets that boast about their burgers being 100 percent pure beef. What they usually mean is 100 percent pure cow. That includes the colon, the intestines, the liver, the kidneys, the spleen—just about everything, in fact. So my advice is, if you are going to eat meat, skip the frozen meat meals like chicken Kiev and stick to organically produced *whole* meats. At least that way you know it is chicken or whatever. When it's encased in breadcrumbs or a pig's intestine, or has a label that it would take a science degree to figure out, it really does become a "mystery food". And speaking of meat . . .

M.E.A.T

Making Elimination Astoundingly Tricky

Before I very briefly cover this subject I would like to put your mind at rest if you are a meat eater—you do not have to stop eating meat altogether to be as healthy as organic wholegrain pie (as long as you skip the mystery stuff). Also, I'm not an anti-meaty. If you want some, feel free. However, like milk, we have been conditioned by many people to believe that meat is not only good for us, but essential. Yes, many people put the fear of God into us by implying we would perish without meat. Well, the truth is that humans can easily live without meat and anyone who tells you otherwise is simply either trying to justify their own meat-eating habits or they have a financial interest in getting you to eat it.

Meat—the red kind in particular—is a super-slow food. It takes an average of four hours for it just to leave the stomach and three days for it to go through the entire system—if you're lucky. If the body is very tired and has a depleted "workforce", some pieces of meat can *stay* in the colon for years—yes years! There it sits, rotting and putrefying—lovely. And the more tired the system becomes, potentially the more rotting red meat is stored. It has been suggested that by the time the average meat eater reaches fifty they'll have two to fourteen pounds of undigested rotting meat in their colon—wonderful!

Meat is also full of saturated fat—another bummer when you consider that heart disease (closely linked to a high intake of saturated fat) is said to kill more people than any other single cause of death (in the U.S.). Meat also has very little fiber and requires lots of staff from your magnificent company to help break it down, assimilate it, and eliminate the waste. However, on the upside, eating plenty of plant food can help this process. *All* plant food on the planet contains oodles of digestive enzymes that have themselves been more or less *predigested* by the plant. This means the enzymes in the plants can be used to help digest meat, thus leaving your enzyme bank account intact (more about that soon).

So, to summarize, if you are going to eat meat, make sure it's non-mystery, and organic where possible, and ensure you eat some "live" (i.e., uncooked) plant food at the same time and/or have a glass of vegetable juice. If you do believe we are natural carnivores (and there are some good reasons to believe so), be aware that *all* carnivores eat their meat raw—only *raw* foods have the life force needed for ultimate health and longevity. I'm not saying eat raw meat, but before you put anything into your mouth it's worth asking yourself . . .

What's Cooking?

Well, not a lot I hope. For many years it has been drummed into our heads that cooked food is perfectly natural and if we don't cook our food we could be swamped with harmful bacteria and potentially become very ill. However, what the experts have failed to tell us is that if you apply enough heat to kill all of the nasty bacteria, you inadvertently kill the good guys too. That means when you overcook your veg, you are literally boiling it to death. The only foods that were ideally designed for human consumption are "live" foods. In fact the only foods meant for any creature on the planet are "live" foods.

**we are the *only* creatures on the planet who cook our food
and we are much worse off for it**

Now before you start thinking I'm anti cooked food and that I never eat the stuff, I want you to know that I'm into nutrition for reality; nutrition for *today's* world—and there's no question that a part of today's world is going out and having cooked dinner with partners and friends. So I'm not going to suggest you eat and drink nothing but raw fruit and veg 24/7—phew! But I am going to suggest that the vast *majority* of what you eat and drink daily is uncooked and therefore very much "alive". I want you to see clearly that when we overkill (cook) our food it becomes lifeless, spent, a total goner.

You Are What You Consume

There is no question that if you drink "dead" liquids and eat "dead" foods, you are not going to feel as alive as you should. Every time you consume processed/cooked foods and drinks you create additional work for your system. I cannot stress enough how important it is to free your digestive system of the constant burden of having to deal with meal after meal of denatured foods and drinks. Dead food simply robs you of life—literally! Dr. Roy Walford has written five books on the subject of immunology and aging and is, as they say, like a farmer— outstanding in his field. Based on his numerous long-term experiments on aging, he is convinced that the human life span should be 120 and we should all arrive there virtually disease free. What interested me particularly was his work on mice. The normal lifespan of mice is about two years, yet Dr. Walford's mice live twice that long. How does he achieve this amazing feat? Simply by freeing up the energy-zapping digestive process for a couple of days every week—pretty amazing don't you think? This illustrates just how important it is to rest your digestive system on a *regular* basis. By *regular*, I don't mean for a few days every New Year—I'm talking here of having predigested-by-the-plant, raw foods and drinks as part of your *daily* diet.

Doing It in the Raw

If you get nothing else from this book please, please do yourself a massive favor by giving your much needed and depleted workforce a holiday from digesting processed foods and drinks. I will be providing much more information about the incredible power of "doing it in the raw" later, but I wanted to touch on it here to begin to counteract the misinformation about cooked food that we've been bombarded with for years. I'm not saying don't have cooked food, far from it, but don't delude yourself into thinking that it's all good for you. Equally, don't now think that *all* cooked food is bad either—it's just the longer you cook something and the higher the temperature, the more lifeless, the more toxic it becomes and thus the harder it is to digest, use, and eliminate. Some natural foods don't just lose their lifeforce but completely change their structure when cooked. Even good old raw carrots are like simple sugars in your bloodstream once cooked. It's one thing cooking food and lowering the nutrient content; it's another to alter it so much from its original state that it turns from food to toxic drug. Yep, there's one "food" (and I really do use the term in its loosest possible sense here) that once consumed will soon have you and your body screaming . . .

Oh Sugar!

Over the last thirty years or so it seems to have become accepted "fact" that fat makes you fat. Fat is viewed as the root of all evil and "no-fat" or "low-fat" products and diets as the means to salvation. However, there's one slight flaw in this theory—it's crap! Don't misunderstand me, I'm not saying that saturated fat is good for you, because it isn't—at all—but our focus needs to shift a bit. The actual amount of fat we consume per head has gone down by about 16 percent since the late 70s, yet obesity has doubled since that time, with an average increase in weight of twelve pounds. *So we are fatter now than when we were consuming more fat.* Here's the spooky thing; the only foodstuffs whose consumption has increased in exact correlation to how fat we're getting are white refined sugar and carbs.

White Refined Sugar and Carbs
or
The Cocaine of the Food World
As I Call It!

Of all the things I talk about, there is no question that white refined sugar and carbs are *by far* the worst. They are highly addictive, highly dangerous, and the biggest single cause of weight gain and diabetes on the planet.

I wish I had the time to go into this subject in depth, but here's a quick summary of what happens when you eat this stuff. When natural food is eaten, it is first broken down in the mouth and then passed into the stomach. Once there it is further broken down and eventually passed into the intestines, where the energy and nutrients can slowly be absorbed. When white refined sugar is eaten, the process is very different. Sugar is "refined" by taking a perfectly natural food that contains a high percentage of sugar and removing all other elements of that food until only the sugar remains. This is then stripped of all vitamins, minerals, proteins, fats, enzymes—in fact *all* nutrients. Because what remains is now an "empty" food, stripped of all fibers and nutrients, it goes straight through the stomach wall *without* being digested, giving an *instant* rush of glucose to the bloodstream. This sends your blood sugar sky high and your body is now in serious trouble. Unless the body lowers your sugar levels fast— you'll die. (So pretty important then.) In response, the body sends one of its team to the pancreas as fast as it can to ask, very nicely of course, if it can have some of the powerful hormone insulin to help lower the sugar levels and regain the body's natural balance. This is the "rush" you get when you have "simple" sugars—it is simply the rush of insulin entering the bloodstream to try and counteract the excess sugar that has just been put in. Here's another problem; the insulin produced to counteract this high blood sugar does its job rather too effectively and causes your sugar levels to *fall*! And when you feel the effects of low blood sugar what do you need? A quick fix. Ummm, see the trap?

Insulin Is the Fat-Producing Hormone

Once the insulin has cleansed the blood of the excess glucose (energy), it needs to get rid of it. What does the body do with this leftover energy? Well some goes into short-term energy storage in the liver, muscles, and so on, but the *majority* will be pushed into long-term storage—that is *fat cells*. If you are one of the many people who struggles with their weight (as I used to), the chances are you're not suffering from "pig-ism" or "greed-ism" (as most people who judge overweight people believe), but have something called "hyperinsulinism", or "Syndrome X". This means that your pancreas has been asked to do too much for too long and is now malfunctioning. The result is that when you eat white sugar and carbs your pancreas now *over-*secretes insulin, and this can often lead to insulin being present in the bloodstream *constantly*. This is a bit of a bugger, as not only is insulin the fat-producing hormone, but when you have insulin in the blood it prevents already-stored fat from being broken down—double whammy! I want to repeat that for all those who struggle to lose weight—

when you have insulin in your bloodstream it not only promotes fat storage but also prevents already-stored fat from being broken down

To make matters worse, it's only when insulin levels drop that we feel truly satisfied. This means that if an overweight person always has some insulin in their blood, not only do they find it incredibly difficult to lose weight but many can never feel truly satisfied, no matter what they eat. This is why I get so annoyed with many nutritionists and dieticians who still promote the, "if you put in more calories than you use up you'll gain weight" nonsense. If you get nothing else from this book please do yourself a massive favor by never counting or taking notice of anything to do with calories ever again. Calorie counting is a meaningless waste of time. The truth is it's simply down to whether your liver over-secretes insulin and whether you have too much insulin in your bloodstream—it's got nothing to do with calories. Calorie counting is misleading hogwash—that much you *do* need to know.

Middle-Age Spread

What this all means, of course, is that if you don't fancy having to battle with your weight or some awful diseases such as diabetes, then skipping white refined sugar *is an absolute must*. I do realize that many people reading this will not have a weight problem; some will even find it hard to gain weight (see Power Smoothies, page 224), but please don't think this doesn't apply to you. We are the only creatures on the planet who suffer from middle-age spread (apart from our pets). Is it possible this happens not because it's a natural part of aging but simply because our workforce gets worn out trying to process all this slow food and can no longer do the job as efficiently? Is it also possible this scenario accounts for the many diseases that we now regard as "normal"? I certainly believe it plays a large part. One thing's for sure though, white refined sugar and carbs (that's refined carbs such as *white* pasta, bread, rice, and such—these all act like sugar in the bloodstream) may be low-fat and some even no-fat, but they over work the pancreas, cause insulin to be loaded into your bloodstream, and make many people fat and ill.

Oh, and don't be misled by "brown sugar" or "raw sugar". Brown sugar is just plain old nasty white sugar that has been dyed, while raw sugar is just white sugar that's missing one of the many refining steps that all sugars go through.

I hope you can now see that avoiding this stuff will make a big contribution to your health. And if you've been battling with your weight for years, it should now be obvious that your problem will not be solved by going fat-free. Your problem will and can *only* be solved by getting rid of white refined sugar and carbs once and for all.

How's This for a Sweetener?

While we're on the subject of sugar, I must quickly mention sweeteners. So many people think they are doing themselves a massive favor by replacing sugar with sweeteners. Please, please, please—if it says "Sugar Free" anywhere on the label, DON'T EVEN THINK ABOUT IT. "Sugar Free" means added sweetener, and *all* sweeteners do about as much for health as the singing chipmunks did for music—nothing. Artificial sweeteners have been linked with symptoms including headaches (the most common), poor vision, depression, panic attacks, *brain tumors*—and, believe it or not, carbohydrate cravings. Yes, these "diet" drinks and foods actually make you crave more of the very things that make you fat. In fact, as Ralph Walton, M.D., Chairman of the Center for Behavioral Medicine states, "If you feed a lab animal aspartame, you wind up with an obese animal". But for me it's the link to brain tumours that's the most worrying. To be fair, sweeteners need a whole book. If you want to know more, read the "Diet Coke Break" chapter in *Slim 4 Life* or log onto www.aspartametruth.com.

The Great Caffeine Con

Another one of those products you would be wise to cut down on or get rid of altogether is caffeine. Caffeine is an incredibly valuable commodity and the reason why it's so profitable is simple—it's a highly addictive drug. The need for any drug is simply created by the drug itself. Before people start drinking caffeine they don't need it; it's only *after* they've had their first couple of hits that the need is created. Now in case you feel you don't actually drink that much coffee so this subject doesn't apply to you, think again. This highly addictive drug is finding its way into many foods and drinks.

A small bar of chocolate, for instance, often contains the same amount of caffeine as a cup of tea or coffee (yep, tea also contains caffeine, often as much as coffee), while "energy drinks" like Red Bull can contain as much caffeine as a cup of strong filtered coffee. And let's not forget the "soft" drinks industry. Not content with loading their liquid nightmares with tons of white refined sugar and chemicals, they want to make them as addictive as possible, and what better way than adding plenty of caffeine—a substance that speeds up the aging process, makes your nerves stand on end, and overworks the liver and kidneys.

There has of course been plenty of "good press" about caffeine, but please let us not forget that some "experts" still say nicotine has many health benefits—oh and they have tests to prove it! Trust me, whenever you hear a report of the "benefits" of caffeine, it's all total bull. The good news is that it only takes forty eight hours for caffeine to leave your bloodstream, and once you have some super, nutrient-packed fast food flowing through your system, the only thing you'll feel is a mild headache, if that.

FAT CHANCE

As you're now aware, many foods have been given good press when they're actually pretty bad. However, there is one food group that has been given an unbelievably bad press when in reality we just couldn't function at all without it—fat. Yes, here's another fact that we *do* need to know—the right kinds of fat are *essential*. So many people think that a "fat-free" diet would solve all their weight problems. The truth is if they went 100 percent fat free, all their problems would be solved—because they would be dead. Have you ever heard of "essential fatty acids"? They don't call them essential for nothing—if we don't get them from our food we die. A certain amount of the right fats in our diet is therefore vital. However, what many people don't realize is that every *natural* food on the planet contains some fat—yes even an apple and a cucumber.

Om-e-ga for You to Know This

The body is quite an ingenious machine, and even if the fats eaten in fruits and vegetables are minimal, the body has the ability to manufacture most of its required fatty acids from fruit and vegetable sugars—clever, eh? However, there are two fatty acids that cannot be manufactured by the body and these go by the wonderful names of omega-6 and omega-3. Omega-6 is pretty much found in most of what you eat already—fruit, veg, legumes, whole grains, and vegetable oils (hmm, perhaps not what you eat already)—so the chances of being deficient in this fat are pretty slim. It's a different story with omega-3 fatty acids—a great many of us don't consume nearly enough of these. Omega-3 fatty acids can be found in cold-water fish such as salmon, sardines, mackerel, herring, tuna, swordfish, and halibut; in seeds such as flaxseed; in hemp and natural, nonroasted nuts; and last but certainly not least—in green leafy vegetables. You can also buy things like Udo's oil, which contains both omega-3 and omega-6 essential fatty acids. This can be used as a salad dressing or simply poured into a juice (it's available from health food stores).

Both the fat we eat and our body fat is extremely important for many purposes. It boosts the immune system, governs our energy metabolism, is used as an emergency energy store, and helps to cushion the joints and protect the muscles. It even plays a part in our sex lives, as we need fat to help make hormones like estrogen and testosterone. Fat also stimulates the brain, so it's hardly surprising that very low fat diets have been linked with depression and other mental disorders. Oh, and one other small point about fat—it contains vital hormones that help to regulate the appetite, yes . . .

fat helps to regulate your appetite

Please remember then that fat is a must in your diet, but make sure it's the *right* kind. Fats from natural sources (with the exception of coconut milk) are what the body needs to thrive—it's the saturated bad stuff you find lurking in soooooo many processed foods that you've got to look out for. And while you're looking, please don't be fooled by anything that says whatever percentage fat free. Bear in mind you can get a two-pound bag of white refined sugar and stick a label on it saying 100 percent fat free, but once the stuff is in your body it will produce plenty of fat.

So let me make myself clear: I'm not anti fat, I'm just anti saturated fat, and I'm not anti sugar either, I'm just anti white refined lifeless sugar. What I am a total fan of, though, are the right kind of fats and the right kinds of sugars. Our brains and bodies need sugar, and most of nature's foods have this wonderful and much-needed fuel in exactly the right amounts to enable our systems to run efficiently.

So it's all pretty black and white then—avoid the crap and get your good sugar and fats from fruit and veg. Well it would be that simple if we could see past all the devious advertising and mislabeling. Now clearly I don't like many of the sweet, chocolate, or fast food giants, but at least the makers of Coke, for example, don't try to kid us that it's actually good for us, they just pay major celebrities massive amounts of money to make their product hip and trendy. But what really gets on my banana are certain foods and drinks that are loaded with the wrong kind of sugar, yet give the impression that they are healthy. There are numerous examples of this, but as this is a book about juicing (yes it is really, we will get there very soon, I promise) I think we should take a few minutes to look at some of the "fruit and veg juices" that aren't quite what they claim to be.

Pure Squeezed Florida Unsweetened Juice

Reading the above, what would you think you're getting? Probably what most people would think—freshly squeezed, unsweetened, pure juice. However, anything with "Florida squeezed" or "Pure squeezed" on the label usually has been juiced abroad, then frozen, and can be as much as six months old (after which time it's got about as much life left in it as a Sunday afternoon game of horseshoes). And anything with "pure unsweetened" written on the label can unbelievably (yet perfectly *legally*), have up to 15g of white refined sugar added per litre to make the juice taste sweeter.

Fruit or Juice "Drinks"

Watch out for this piece of trickery: "fruit drinks" or "juice drinks" can contain as little as 5 percent actual fruit juice. The rest can be made up with water, white sugar or sweeteners (such as Aspartame) and other artificial additives worthy of any decent "mystery drink" convention. Most of these so-called fruit drinks have a much, much larger percentage of sugar and chemicals than juice. Yet despite this, they're often refrigerated in supermarkets—I assume to encourage people to believe they're fresh. The truth is many of these "fruit juice drinks" have not only been pasteurized, which prolongs shelf life, but also contain loads of sugar and chemicals, which makes it completely unnecessary to keep them cold.

Enriched with Added Vitamins and Minerals

Oh, how kind of them, they care about our health so much that they've "enriched" our drinks with "added vitamins and minerals" . . . or have they? Well yes and no really. It's true that they *do* add some—nearly always *synthetic*—vitamins and minerals to their juices, but make no mistake; in no way, shape, or form does this make them healthy. Labels that make such claims are usually on drinks (often those aimed at children) that contain white refined sugar and chemicals. To my mind, adding *synthetic* vitamins and minerals to liquid that is laced with sugar, additives, and chemicals is equivalent to putting a gilt frame around a "paint by number" and calling it a masterpiece. And why do they feel the need to add vitamins and minerals anyway—shouldn't there be plenty of naturally occurring vitamins and minerals in there already? The same applies when you see labels bragging, "no artificial colors, flavourings, sweeteners, and preservatives". This once again gives the impression they've done something good, but they shouldn't be adding them in the first place, should they?

Fresh Organic Juice

The word "organic" is now appearing on just about everything, but "organic" doesn't necessarily make it good. After all you can no doubt get some organic cocaine! When it comes to juice, the word "organic" is only of significance if the juice is "freshly extracted" i.e., made in front of you either at home or in a juice bar—otherwise you can be sure that it's been heat-treated. And of course if it has, you really are paying through the nose for nothing. My advice is, if you want an organic juice while you're out, hunt down a juice bar.

Time to Stop Concentrating

You've probably heard certain companies promoting their juice by saying it's "not from concentrate", but what does "concentrate" really mean? Concentrating juice involves heating the juice to a very high temperature in order to remove the excess water content and help prolong shelf life. The main problem with this is that it gains "shelf life" but has no "life" left in it. I must repeat this point again—when you apply heat to foods or liquids, you immediately lower the enzyme activity. What that means is you kill some of its "life force"; the higher the temperature the more life force you lose. If a juice has a shelf life of more than forty eight hours you can be pretty sure the vast majority of the nutrients are dead, and this also goes for the "not from concentrate" brigade—so watch out.

100% Pure Juice
Sweet and Fairly Innocent

Even the 100 percent pure juice brands out there, such as Juicy Juice and Apple & Eve, have also been heat-treated. However, the labels on their juices saying, "made with 100 percent pure juice" are among the few that *don't* lie. These juices are indeed made with nothing but fruit juice. However—yes there's a however—in order for the juice to have such a long shelf life it does have to be heated in some manner, and when you apply heat, you inevitably kill the life. So even with the 100 percent pure juice versions, please don't delude yourself into thinking you're getting 100 percent "live" nutrition, because you just aren't, I'm afraid. (I'm currently working on something called "The Juice Master's Complete" and it will be the only "live" complete vegetable juice on the market, so keep a look out in a store near you.) However, if you're on the go and you really just want something more than water, then these genuine 100 percent pure fruit juices are the *only* ones to get. They may be pretty dead on the 'live' front, but they're in a completely different league to the white refined sugar-, additive-, and chemical-laced fruit juices that are to be found lurking on the shelves and they do still of course contain some vitamins and natural sugars.

One thing for sure though, and what you "do need to know" is *every time* you consume "dead" foods and drinks in the absence of pure "live" nutrition, you slowly but surely weaken your workforce and make withdrawals from your body bank account of health. It is highly likely you've been left with excess fat stored around many parts of your body; battered organs; elevated sugar levels; a weakened ticker; a very depleted "life" bank account; a clogged colon; waste matter circulating in your bloodstream, veins, and arteries; and possibly arthritis, asthma, or diabetes. You will also probably have sticky blood cells and very low energy levels. In fact, we have clogged our systems so much over the years that there is a good chance that your colon has a buildup of waste matter that has gradually hardened and stuck to its walls over the years, reducing what is normally a six-centimeter wide tunnel to one as small as just a few millimeters. Or, in other words, it's like trying to shove a watermelon through a Lifesaver! We are now—

THE MOST CONSTIPATED GENERATION IN WORLD HISTORY WITH 147,000 NEW CASES OF COLORECTAL CANCER EVERY YEAR!

There is however, some magnificent news, no matter how full of it you are, whatever state your health account is in, or however tired your workforce, it's *never* too late to start reinvesting in your health/longevity account and reaping the unbelievable daily rewards of a brand new workforce and unclogged system. And, as mentioned at the beginning, it's spookily easy to replenish those accounts—all you need is the *right* currency and the ultimate in nutrient delivery system technology. And to my mind there is simply only one currency suitable for an *already* beaten up and clogged digestive system and only one super vehicle to deliver it—yep, it's time to crack open your savings account and pour in some . . .

4

Pure Liquid Gold

Over 95 percent of the planet is made up of it (72 percent of its surface), over 70 percent of our bodies are made up of the stuff, and life as we know it just wouldn't exist without it—so, I don't really think you need to be Sherlock Holmes to figure out the foods ideally meant for human consumption are the ones loaded with life-giving, body-cleansing, refreshing water. And, as you just may have guessed, there are only two kinds of food that really fit the bill—good old fruit and veg. In fact, there just isn't one single fruit or vegetable on the planet that we humans consume that doesn't contain at least 70 percent water—some even reaching a whopping 99 per cent.

How's Your Health Bank Account?

The water contained in ripe *raw* fruit and colorful veg is unlike any other liquid on the planet. It is loaded with what can only be described as pure liquid gold, and it is this liquid—contained in *all* nature's super fast foods—that can replenish your depleted bank account of life. What do I mean? We are each born with a quota of enzymes (our bank account of life), and we can either add to that account (by eating raw, whole foods in the form of juices) or deplete it (for instance, through consuming alcohol, processed foods, etc). Every time you eat a burger, have a coffee, or consume any kind of junk foods and drinks, your body has to dip into its "life" (enzyme) account and make a withdrawal. The more withdrawals you make, the poorer you become. The problem is we are talking here about your "life" account, the single most important account you will ever own, and unless you deposit some liquid gold on a daily basis then you won't end up financially poor, but far more importantly, mentally, physically, and emotionally poor. This can manifest itself in all kinds of ways: headaches, lethargy, rapid aging, a clogged system, stored fat, heart disease, cancer, diabetes, arthritis, and asthma—to name but a few. And if you keep spending your "life" bank account as if there's no tomorrow, then the chances are there really will be no tomorrow. If you go into the red on this account, I'm afraid the show's over!

The good news is that replenishing your life account is easy—simply furnish your body on a daily basis with pure liquid gold from fresh fruit and veg. As yet, we have no way of knowing *exactly* what it is in fruit and veg that makes them so remarkable when it comes to our health and longevity, but one thing is for certain, the vast majority of the "X" factor is to be found in the super-nutrient-charged liquid they contain. It is this "live" liquid that makes *all* raw fruits and colorful veg the super-fast, super-rich, antidisease, health-giving foods that they are.

We're Not All Uncle Fred

Have you ever wondered why some people eat and drink rubbish all their lives yet still live relatively long, seemingly healthy and happy lives? First of all, a true "Uncle Fred" story—you know the one where "he ate, drank and smoked everything yet never had one day's illness in his life"—is very rare (often they're made up or grossly exaggerated). The truth is the vast (and I do mean *vast*) majority of people in the Western world *do* die prematurely and *do* suffer from ill health. In fact, the number of people who now die of genuine, natural causes is so low that it's not even registered any more. People who manage to come thorough life unscathed by an unhealthy lifestyle are simply born with one hell of an enzyme/life bank account. The problem is such people don't leave much of a legacy for the next generation. Let me explain . . .

Pottenger's Cats — Raw vs Cooked

One Dr. Frances Pottenger conducted a very thorough experiment using 900 cats. The test was simple and involved feeding the cats two types of food—raw and cooked. The cats fed only on raw food had healthy offspring year after year and suffered no ill health, disease, or premature death. They only died as a result of old age. However, the cats fed on *cooked* food (this was exactly the same food as the first group, only cooked) developed every one of humanity's modern ailments—heart disease, cancer, arthritis, kidney disease, pneumonia, loss of teeth, diarrhea, behavior change (so much so that the cats became dangerous to handle), lack of sexual desire, osteoporosis, liver problems, and so on.

However, the crunch for all those "Uncle Freds" out there comes when the cats' offspring were examined. The first group, the "living" food cats, gave birth to healthy kittens year after year. For the second group, the cooked-food cats, it was a very different story. Some of first generation of kittens born to this group showed signs of abnormalities and illnesses. By just the second generation many were born diseased or dead—and by the third generation many of the mothers were sterile. This means that although Uncle Fred may have inherited a fab enzyme account, he was using up the inheritance for the next. He ate, drank, and smoked everything, but every time he did he was using up his enzyme inheritance, leaving little, if anything, for the next generation.

It now seems perfectly "natural" for babies to be born with all kinds of disease. I don't believe the majority of cases are natural or normal. Clearly some of them are, and I'm not saying for one second that all babies born with disease are a result of what their parents or grand-parents consumed; that clearly is not the case, but there's no question that more and more children are being born into ill health and science has yet to pinpoint exactly why.

The good news, however, is that when Dr. Pottenger changed the diet of his cooked-food cats back to raw, live, natural foods, the following generations became healthy and disease free. This means that no matter how shot we believe our system to be, once you supply the correct enzyme-rich fuel, the body will soon regenerate and repair.

Enzymes = Life

In case you're wondering what the hell an enzyme is, let me make it simple—ENZYMES ARE LIFE. Without what are called metabolic and digestive enzymes I wouldn't be able to write this book—in fact I wouldn't be able to do anything. Every single activity that takes place in your body requires these wonderful catalysts. Without them you couldn't yawn, blink, spit, blow your nose, or breathe. So whenever I say enzyme I mean life, and it's why I often refer to your enzyme/life account. There is no question that the X amount of metabolic enzymes that we are born with will run out. There is, after all, one sure thing about life—it ain't gonna last forever, no matter what we eat and how many times we clean our auras and chakras. But one thing is certain, pending fatal accidents, YOU will certainly live longer if the majority of what goes into your body is 'living" foods and drinks. That sounds like a pretty bold statement, but it's one I believe to be true. I don't know if you'll live longer than all Uncle Freds—after all, we now know that depends on their particular account—but you will certainly live longer than you would have had you not stopped dipping into your enzyme account.

Much more importantly, the *quality* of your daily life will be vastly improved if you eat "live" foods. From personal experience I know that it's a much, much better life when you're living in a slim, healthy, energy-driven body than an overweight, sluggish, and diseased one. There are many people who are kept alive until 70/80/90, but often when you look at their life they actually stopped "living" in their fifties. My role models are people like the great pioneer of juicing—Dr. Norman

Walker. He died peacefully in his sleep, disease free, at the age of 113. Another U.S. doctor whose diet also consisted of large quantities of "live" juice died at the younger age of ninety six, but in his case the cause of death was being hit by a freak wave while surfing—yep, surfing at ninety six years of age!

Living Foods = Life/Dead Foods = Death

It seems so obvious, yet due to mental conditioning, there are many individuals, experts, and government bodies who say that you *must* have cooked food—that you cannot live on living foods. How barking mad is that? Are they a few burners short of a full stove? All "living" foods have enzymes and enzymes equal LIFE! Every time we eat "live" foods we can rest assured that we don't have to deplete our enzyme accounts to try and process it—the plant has done the work for us. Not only that, but all living foods contain oodles of enzymes that will help the body deal with disease, build up a defence against ailments, and enable it to deal with any cooked and processed food we *do* eat. Because yes, I live in today's real world and so do you—we have all come to enjoy cooked food, and it is also a huge part of our social life, so I'm not suggesting you turn into a "raw fooder". What I am saying is the more live foods you eat, the more alive you will feel—the more "dead" food you consume, the more like death you will feel.

The Dead Food Hangover

Every day most people are waking up with a food and drink hangover caused by dead, processed food and drink. And because this happens to most people, how on earth is anyone meant to know that it isn't a natural way to feel? After all, those who wake up full of the joys of spring are considered freaks (of the health variety), so when the majority of the population are waking up "feeling like death" it appears natural. It also appears perfectly natural to "use" some kind of quick-fix food or drink to try and rev up the system ready for the day. But the system shouldn't need revving up—it's been resting for six to eight hours and should be bursting with energy. The reason why most people aren't waking up "awake" is because the body hasn't been resting at all. All night long, the body has been working its socks off trying to deal with the previous day's enzyme-free rubbish. It will do its level best to convert what you have put in into usable fuel and do whatever it can to throw out the waste. And if you drink loads of alcohol, have no water, and eat dead foods just before you go to bed, then you will certainly feel more like death than "normal" when you wake up. But, as I will repeat, even what you have come to regard as normal or natural is still usually a hung-over state—it's simply that it has become so familiar it feels like your natural state.

Once again, exactly how hungover you feel will depend on your enzyme bank account. Children, for example, are born with a full account and tend to wake up quite buoyant—even if everything they consumed the day before was as dead as your average Sunday dinner. However, after many years of trying to deal with dead/lifeless foods and drinks, the body begins to process it less efficiently due to the constant backlog and the fact that it has fewer enzymes to do the job. This means you should never compare yourself to other people to gauge your state of health—it all depends on *your* account and *your* inheritance. Instead you need to compare how you feel now to how you *could* feel if you freed up energy currently used to digest dead foods and, in addition, supplied your body with plenty of pure live liquid gold.

Waking Up to the Very Things That Are Making You Tired

What most people don't realize is that the reason they feel so wiped out a lot of the time is because of the empty junkie foods and drinks they're consuming—the very same ones that *appear* to wake them up! People everywhere are reaching for "false" stimulants like caffeine, nicotine, white refined sugars, and so on first thing in the morning in an attempt to get over their junk food and drink hangover and get a bit of life in them. What they don't realize, as I didn't for God knows how many years, is that they could *easily* feel awake and alive the majority of the time if they simply stopped having this stuff on a regular basis. Every time people consume junk foods and drinks, they're trying to reach some kind of equilibrium—they're trying to feel as awake, as satisfied, as fulfilled as people who are not hooked on this stuff, i.e., the people they will often refer to health freaks! Most people are now in a position where they genuinely feel that without these "stimulants" they would feel below par all the time and that these foods and drinks are of huge benefit to them—they view them as something that keeps them going. But it's just one huge trick. They only feel so crappy *because of* the effects of these dead foods and drinks—if they got rid of them they would soon experience a genuine and consistent level of energy, not the roller-coaster ride that results from these sorts of stimulants.

Eric Schlosser, the brilliant author of the bestselling book *Fast Food Nation*, when talking about gambling, stated, "It is the ultimate consumer technology, designed to manufacture not a tangible product, but something much more elusive: a brief sense of hope. That is what Las Vegas really sells, the most brilliant illusion of all, a loss that feels like winning". And as far as I'm concerned this is exactly what the drug, food, and drink industries are doing too. They are selling a *brief* sense of hope, a *moment* where people feel slightly better than they did a second ago, giving the false impression that these products are their best friends and actually help them through the stresses and strains of life. The drug, dead food, and drink industry are selling "empty" nutrition and through clever "hip and trendy" advertising—empty promises. The problem is when you *initially* consume them you do feel *more* awake, *more* alive, and happier than you did a second ago. This is without question the most brilliant illusion of them all, every time you consume junkie-type foods and drinks you clearly lose—but it *feels* like you've just won! That's called addiction. We are now so used to masking the indicators that we've actually reached the stage where if we do get a warning from the body, like a headache or indigestion, we now think our problem is caused by either an aspirin deficiency or we're simply low on Tums!

So it's time to replenish your account and start "living" as opposed to surviving. And to do this, you need one simple tool—pure liquid gold. Good rest, deep breathing, water, and sunshine help, but the pure liquid gold found in fresh, raw fruits and vegetables is the single most important commodity in the world when it comes to health.

"Let Food Be Thy Medicine"

Hippocrates, the so-called "father of medicine", knew only too well the incredible power of raw fruit and veg. "Let food be thy medicine" was perhaps his most well-known saying, and he was certainly right on the button—especially when you consider that what people put into their mouths is the biggest cause of death on the planet *by far*. The body can only function as it should if it has the time and the workforce (i.e., the necessary enzymes) to do so. However, it spends so much time and energy trying to digest the rubbish we put in it that it simply doesn't have the time or energy to shift things like excess fat, repair damaged organs, or give us the mental or physical vibrancy we crave. If we just learned to "free up" energy in the body and provide it with the workforce it needs, then the actual physical side of getting a slim, healthy, energy-driven body is very, very easy. The body just needs some help—and fast, nutrient-rich food is what it's crying out for.

The Elixir of Life

I will repeat this point once more: the human body was designed with only one kind of food in mind—fast! And once again, I don't mean burgers and fries. I mean foods flowing with bundles of "live" nutrients and organic water, making them easy and *fast* to digest, *fast* for your body to assimilate and *fast* for the body to eliminate. Fruit and green, leafy veg require little or no digestion and so leave the stomach very quickly, usually in about thirty minutes (remember, meat takes four hours). They then go straight to the intestines, where the energy and nutrients can be absorbed.

Fruit requires no washing up, tastes wonderful, looks amazing, satisfies a *genuine* hunger, is cheap compared to most things, and the high liquid gold content helps to transport the life-giving nutrients to every cell in the body and flush the system of waste matter. Pretty incredible stuff! Yet nine times out of ten, humans get hold of these truly magnificent live foods, stick them in a pan, cook out the juice, cook out the life, cover it with loads of drug-like sugar, sprinkle on some "mystery" bits of colorful what looks like small splinters, give it some pretentious French name and call themselves "master" chefs.

Anyone with any shred of common sense can see clearly that *raw* fruits and green leafy vegetables are the foods above any other that we are biologically adapted to eat. They are the easiest to digest, use, create very little waste, and are high in life-giving water, and they also contain all the stuff needed for supreme health and longevity. However, if cooking is processing and if nature produces our foods in the *exact* ratio needed for amazing health and vitality, and given nature has packaged our food in such a convenient way, then you may well be asking . . .

5
Why Juice, Mr. Juice Master?

 Above all others, the most commonly asked question I get is "If you're into food 'as nature intended', why not just eat your fruit and veg rather than juicing them?" Yes, I agree, at first glance juicing doesn't appear very natural at all, and if we had been eating nothing but nature's intended food since the day we were born and had no intention of ever eating anything else for the rest of our lives, then without question there would be no need to juice. However, we have a problem, Houston! The typical Western diet takes its toll on the body, and chances are you now have one hell of a clogged, weak, and fairly lifeless system. Years upon years of the wrong sorts of foods will almost certainly have left their mark, and it is more than probable, nay it's a certainty, that at this stage you will have a "pm, Friday, holiday weekend situation" going on. What? Let me explain . . .

Imagine being on the freeway on a Friday afternoon, holiday weekend, heading for the country. Do you see lots of flowing traffic or an almighty jam? Exactly. Now, no matter how much you want to get to where you're going faster, the heavy traffic ahead of you will be preventing you from getting there.

Now transfer this scenario to your digestive system. Years upon years of "food stuffs" sticking to the walls of your colon (and other places!) can mean the once wide tunnel of your colon can have closed to just a few millimeters—creating one hell of a jam. This means that it's very likely that even if you *do* eat some good stuff it's still going to take a while to get through the built-up traffic to the many, probably starving, cells that are crying out for it. That is, of course, if it makes it there at all. If fruit or veg cannot make their way through, they have a tendency to rot in the gut while they wait. Many people who say fruit and veg don't agree with them are simply eating it in the freeway holiday weekend situation and often have the wonderful fumes to prove it!

What's needed is the "freeway am, Christmas morning situation"—a beautiful clear and empty road. But in order to get the lanes free and flowing again, and to avoid the "stick a hose up your bottom and suck as hard as you can" colonic approach (takes all sorts—don't know about you, but mine's got a massive no-entry sign on it!), we need to somehow bypass the rotting dead food traffic jam and get the super-powered workforce to where it's needed. And how do we do that? We use . . .

The Super-Fast Nutrient Courier

And yes—as you've probably guessed by now—life-giving, energy-releasing, raw fruit and vegetable juices are without question the fastest and single most powerful way to get live nutrients through your clogged system and into every cell in your body. It's like having a super-fast nutrient courier bike that can weave in and out of all the built-up traffic to deliver the liquid life force directly to where it's needed. So if you want a surefire way to ensure your cells get fed the "live" nutrients they need *every day* in the fastest and most efficient way it's time to get juiced!

Juicing is a truly masterful way of supplying your body with the liquid gold it's been crying out for—in the fastest possible time, without the energy-zapping digestive process. Remember, it takes more energy to digest and process food than virtually any other activity, and it takes *energy* to get a slim and healthy body. If you already have a clogged, fat, tired, and ill system, your body can do with all the help it can get on the digestion front, and sending your nutrients on the juice express is a guaranteed way of freeing up that energy and really feeding your cells with the least hassle.

We Are Just One Big Juicing Machine

Eating raw fruit and veg in its original state is a natural thing to do —but so too is juicing. Many experts will argue with that, but what they don't seem to realize is that we, like all animals on the planet, already have the most efficient juice extractor contained within— we are in fact just one large juice extractor. The only problem is our machine hasn't been cleaned for a very long time. This is why a juice extractor is so wonderful; the machine does the work that your body normally has to. It takes whole fruits and veg and miraculously extracts the pure liquid gold that is so easy for the body to digest and assimilate.

Fruit and green leafy veg are, in themselves, very easy for the body to digest and are themselves super-fast foods. But what makes juicing them so wonderful for an already tired and abused workforce is that it takes even *less* work and time for the body to get what it needs from the juice. Also, given the "freeway holiday situation", the body now actually receives *more* of the liquid gold into the cells when in juice form than if you were to eat the fruit and veg in their natural casing. When we *eat* vegetables and fruits, the body uses energy trying to squeeze the liquid it needs from the fibers, then it has to find the energy to chuck out the leftovers. Guess what? When you put fruit and veg through a juicing machine, you've effectively done the body's work for it. The "chute" or "feeder" is the neck; the main crushing/spinning part is the stomach, the "pulp" is the leftovers (that would come out anyway!) and the juice extracted is the PURE LIQUID GOLD. By drinking freshly extracted juice, you have skipped the digestive process and effectively furnished your cells with tons of live, raw nutrients—brilliant!

Besides, even if you did eat nature's finest all your life, a juice extractor would still be of huge benefit to you. What many people don't know is that although the body is pretty good at breaking down fruit and green leafy veg, it finds vegetables like carrots, broccoli, beetroot, swede, and such a little more tricky. These veg contain tremendous amounts of liquid gold, but the body can have a pretty tough time trying to internally "juice" hard vegetables, especially when it is already tired and weak. This is why we tend to steam or cook them—to make them easier to digest. The problem with this, as you now know, is that when you apply any kind of heat, you effectively kill a large percentage of the live nutrients and at the same time *increase* the waste that needs to be disposed of. Juicing is a completely different ball game. The man-made juice extractor breaks down the hard veg for you, then sucks out the live nutrition and puts it in a liquid form that is just soooooo easy for the body to use.

You Cannot Live on Juice Alone

Let me make something quite clear—while I'm perhaps the world's biggest juicing fan, I'm not saying don't ever *eat* fruits or veg, in fact, quite the opposite. *Whole* fruits and green leafy veg in particular are pretty easy for the body to digest, even for a battered system, and all whole fruit and veg contain fiber, without which you really would be in trouble. No man or woman can live, nor should live, on juice alone—juicing is a tool, not a rule. It's an amazing catalyst to get you to the land of the slim and healthy—and keep you there. A couple of glasses of juice a day is not only delicious, it not only helps to feed the entire body, but is the ultimate health insurance policy. It's much, much easier to prevent disease than it is to try and cure it. When you make a juice, you are not simply making a creamy, delicious, scrumptious drink—you are creating the ultimate health tonic packed full of vitamins, minerals, the right sugars, the right fats, water, protein, and of course bio-blooming-flavinoids! And no pill or potion on any shelf in any pharmacy anywhere in the world can come close to the magical powers contained in that glass of liquid gold.

A few years ago a company called Pure Juice had an idea to open juice bars in all the mainline train stations throughout the U.K.; the pilot juice bar was in Paddington. The juices made were all organic and were just simply wonderful. As I used to travel from Birmingham to London several times a week, I used to make a point of stopping at the station just to get a freshly extracted organic juice. The bar folded within a year and the chain never happened—why? For one reason, what people *thought* they were getting was just an expensive fruit or vegetable drink, when in reality, they were getting the best life giver and disease preventative in the world, and what price would you put on that? I mean, how much is your heart worth? What about your liver? Kidneys? Eyesight? What about your life? How much would you give someone to cure cancer if you had it? What about heart disease? I don't know about you, but I'd remortgage my house and even sell my mother . . .'s house to find the cure. This may not be a cure once someone has *already* got horrific diseases, but by Jiminy, liquid gold is the best life giver and disease preventer on the planet, and in my book, if it cost ten dollars a glass—I'd find the money!

Police Feel Free to Be Radical

I've already stated that your body is like a massive organization with many different departments; in reality it's more like a complete society with all within it working together in perfect harmony. However, just like any society, there's always going to be those who want to spoil the party; you know, those radical types who want to be free to cause mayhem. Unless you have some kind of structure within any society you'll have complete anarchy—and one place you certainly don't want anarchy is inside the very unique society known as—your body. But unless you have some liquid gold going in on a daily basis, there is no question: you'll have several riots breaking out and looting will be rife!

Ever heard of something called "free radicals"? The answer is probably yes, but do you know what they are? Well, I could say, "a free radical is an atom or group of atoms containing at least one unpaired electron, which, wanting to be paired, steal electrons from other pairs", or I could simply say that free radicals are the scavengers doing the looting and causing the riots. Free radicals have been implicated in the development of diseases such as cancer and heart disease. Right now—yes, this minute as you read this page—these life suckers are creating all kinds of mayhem in many different parts of your body—not a nice thought. However, there is a special free radical police force specially designed to restore order.

Fight "O" Nutrients

Antioxidants, now there's a name—heard of the term? Know what they are? Well, to put it in a way that's mind-blowingly easy to understand, they are simply a special task force designed to help curb free radical damage and restore balance and order within our bodies—or "free radical police" as I call them. Do you know the best place to find these free radical police? Yep, you guessed it—fruit and veg (well cover me in liquid iron and hit me with a hammer!). All fruits and veg contain something called phytonutrients; I call them the S.A.S (Super Antioxidant Service) of the health world—a crack squad sent in to restore order.

All sorts of things cause free radical damage—poor air quality, stress and even too much exercise—it's not all solely due to poor diet. Free radical activity is quite normal and happens in all animals—the difference is that wild animals usually have the necessary tools (i.e. a decent antioxidant police force) to deal with it. Most humans in Western society have a free radical police force that's on its knees and needs new recruits—fast!

eat **your fruits and veg and the free radical police will help out when they can** ***drink*** **them and they'll be on the scene before you can say chemotherapy!**

Many authorities are now convinced that free radicals kick off the cancer process; *all agree* free radicals are a real danger. Dr. Gladys Block, of the University of California at Berkeley, reviewed 170 studies from seventeen nations and concluded that people everywhere who eat the most fruits and veg, compared with those who eat the least, slash their chances of getting cancer by up to 50 percent. But again, like any study, there can always be arguments against, and there are just so many contributing factors to disease it's often hard to judge any study. However, one study, if you can call it that, is undisputed. *All wild animals from every single area of the globe eat their foods "live"* and the percentage that suffers degenerative disease and obesity is less than 5 percent—coincidence? Well, I for one don't think so.

It's a Double Rollover!

For your body, a *daily* helping of super-fast food is the equivalent of the largest ever lottery win. The biggest difference with this lottery is that all you have to do is buy your juicing ticket every day, and you're guaranteed to win. But the prize this time is health, energy, and physical and mental vibrancy. That's something no amount of money can ever buy. No matter how financially rich you are, if you're overspending on your enzyme account, you cannot simply transfer funds to get out of the red—once you've spent it, you're spent too. In terms of sheer quality of our daily lives, we need to replenish our enzyme account *every day* and keep our free radical police force in fine fettle.

I'm not exaggerating when I say that juicing is quite simply liquid gold for your body and mind. Every time you have a glass of freshly extracted fruit and vegetable juice you will just feel the goodness pouring through your system within minutes. And the taste of the juice you make yourself is in a different league from the nutritionally dead versions you see on supermarket shelves masquerading as the real thing. Even vegetable juice, when made in the right way, tastes like one of the Seven Wonders of the World.

The fact is most people have never tasted the rich, creamy liquid sunshine you get from fresh, just-juiced vegetables. The only vegetable juice most people have tried is carrot, and this is usually the denatured version found on supermarket shelves. To be fair, when it comes to vegetable juices, it's the idea more than anything that's off-putting— they just sound, well, AWFUL! And many people, if they don't know what they're doing, will have that impression confirmed with the first vegetable concoction they make. Some of the versions I have tried tasted a few rats short of sewer water. But I can assure you, if you're willing to be adventurous, when you taste just how rich, smooth, and creamy they *can* be (the Juice Master way), you'll be converted for life.

I remember doing a juicing road show around the U.K. and watching parents' disbelieving faces as they saw their children drinking raw vegetable juice—and loving it. I'll never forget one woman who said, "Oh my God, my son is drinking vegetables," then continued by saying, "No, you don't understand—MY SON IS DRINKING VEGETABLES!" I've never been to one of those "healing seminars," but by her reaction you would have thought I'd just made her son walk again.

To be honest, though, even if vegetable juices did taste disgusting, given the amazing change in my weight and health, I would just hold my nose and pour the stuff down. Fortunately, they do taste incredible, and even the ones I initially found a bit weird, I now love.

The Juice Master Taste Gym

Over a remarkably short period of time, the brain and body can learn to adjust to and get to love any food or drink consumed on a regular basis (though I would argue this doesn't apply to Brussels sprouts). If you don't believe that's true, just think how your first-ever alcoholic drink tasted—yep it sucked! But, and here's the point, even though it tasted awful, you soon got to like it—and that's fruit and vegetation that's gone bad. By comparison, learning to enjoy nature's finest vegetable juice is a piece of kiwi cake, again, as long as they're made in the right—Juice Master—way. So even if you find you don't absolutely adore your first vegetable juice, rest assured your taste buds will adjust and in no time at all you'll find you love them. A lot of people love them from the start, but even if they don't make you leap in the air shouting, "juice me baby—juice me baby" from the beginning, just put yourself into The Juice Master's Taste Gym for a couple of weeks and in no time at all you'll be singing their praises.

The Future's Bright, the Future's Green

The reason I'm so keen to get you into vegetable juices is because in terms of sheer nutritional value, veg juice reigns supreme. Don't get me wrong, fruit juices are great, but you can overdo fruit juice and they *can*, unless you are careful, cause unnecessary sugar imbalances (more on this later). Vegetable juices, on the other hand, are just sunshine to your cells—literally. All dark green veg like broccoli, spinach, cucumber, wheatgrass, kale, and so on contain something called chlorophyll (nice name). This stuff traps the energy of sunlight and when the plant is broken down, the life-giving energy is released. When you juice green veg you are effectively making yourself a cup of sunshine—how wonderful is that? And that cup of sunshine is the most valuable form of carbohydrate there is. The antioxidants and chloro-whatsit found in vegetables all help to drastically decrease our chances of getting cancer, heart disease, and God knows what else.

This is all fine and dandy, but for most of us the idea of sitting down to a plateful of raw broccoli, kale, spinach, celery, beetroot, ginger, and carrots, doesn't exactly make us want to do somersaults in the snow. In fact, the average person's daily intake of raw, live nutrition in the form of fruit and veg is somewhere between 0 and 5 per cent—that pretty much equals suicide. This is where juicing comes to the rescue. It's a very neat way of replenishing your enzyme account in the fastest possible way without having to *eat* lots of raw veg.

Green with Envy

One of my mentors is Jay Kordich—the juice man. This man looks fantastic; not "fantastic for his age"—he just looks fantastic. He is well known for his statement, "All life on earth emanates from the *green* of the plant." The late Dr. Bircher-Benner, who founded the famous Bircher-Benner clinic said, "There is nothing more therapeutic on earth than green juice." Make no mistake, if there was ever a time to go green, it is now. As I've said, fruit juices are fab, and fruit smoothies are just heaven on your taste buds, but it's the green juices that really supply pure sunshine to every cell in your body in the fastest way possible, and make a truly unbelievable impact on your health, looks, and energy levels—which really can make others green with envy!

"Save Your Life, Change Your Life"

Jack La Lanne is an eighty seven-year-old food/health/fitness/juicing guru. You may well have seen him selling his juicer on shopping TV. The juicer, in my opinion, may not be anything super-special, but the man certainly is. He is known as The Godfather of Fitness—and for good reason. This guy is almost super-human. Among other amazing feats, when he was sixty he pulled a 1000 pound boat across the San Antonio river—while his hands were cuffed and legs shackled! He is completely convinced that juicing is the key to his vitality and vibrancy. He wakes up at 5:30 every morning and works out for two hours a day. That may well be your idea of hell, but whether you would *want* to or not, wouldn't it be nice to know you *could*—especially at eighty seven years of age? Jack La Lanne's catch phrase is simple, "Save your life, change your life." In his words, "if you put juice in your body today, you'll have a much better tomorrow." And oh my, as I can personally vouch, he's right. He is convinced juicing saved and changed his life—and it can do the same for yours.

Juicing is without question the key to unlocking your mental and physical vibrancy. If, even after all you've read here, you still don't believe me, just become your own guinea pig and see, live, and *feel* the results—you will never look back. OK, so some scientists would say my theories on juicing are "un-scientific", but who cares as long as it works? Who cares *how* it works, as long as it works? The only reason you have picked up a book of this nature is to improve your health, and no matter how good or how bad you think your diet has been, you can *always* raise your health to the next level—even if you've already read *Slim 4 Life*. As I mentioned at the start, so many people *talk* great health and can tell you what to do to have incredible health, but very few actually walk the talk. They say one thing out loud, then go and secretly eat their way through loads of dead junkie food when no one is looking (yep, I've been there!).

If you've been a talker for a while, it's time to make your health number one priority and start walking the talk. And, as I promised, it's easy. This is where most people get it wrong; they think it's difficult to eat healthily. In truth the difficult part is *not* making the change; the real heartache is *not* having some juice in your life.

Time to Get Mentally and Physically Juiced

If you've fully understood what I've been saying, you should be itching like Lord Itch of Itching Hall in Itching to get started, but wait! I don't want you going off running on enthusiasm without any guidance; after all, you have no clue how to make a juice at the moment. Most people run on short-lived enthusiasm when they start juicing. They may have read about juicing in a magazine, so they buy a machine, make some awful juice that takes an eternity and then say, "Oh, sod that for a game of soldiers," and stick the machine in a cupboard never to see the light of day again. To avoid this, I'm going to tell you how to set up a "juice kitchen" so it becomes part of your *daily* life, how to make a juice super-fast, what machines to buy, and, of course, provide you with some fab recipes and all the information you'll ever need about the fruit and veg suitable for juicing.

But before all that I want to give you some Juice Master guidance on the best time to furnish your system with liquid gold, some tips on "how to drink it" and a page dedicated to fully understanding fruit sugars and their effects on your health and internal balance.

This first piece of advice I regard as the most important. I deal with the real world, and in the real world it can be all too easy to get caught up, get too tired and reach the "I can't be bothered" stage. With that in mind, and to make sure you reap the incredible benefits of having at least one BIG glass of freshly extracted juice a day, it's time to . . .

6

Get up and Get Juiced

When you get up in the morning what's the first room you usually visit? Yep, the bathroom—why? Because you're bursting to go and you stink. As you can see, I haven't read "how to win friends and influence people," but come on, I'm a realist, and in reality *most* people wake up with their hair stuck together, sleep in their eyes, smelly armpits, a mouth that feels like the inside of Gandhi's flip-flop, and breath straight from Satan's bottom! However, this is a good thing. Now it may not seem it as your partner nearly kills you from the gust of the words "good morhhhhhhhning," but, as the old saying goes . . .

Better out Than in

The more toxic food and drink you consume, the more energy the body expends trying to use it and the more toxins the body chucks out—simple equation really. This is why after someone has had a good skinful of alcohol and eaten loads of mystery food on the back of it (after all alcohol came first—kebabs second!) they will wake up more sweaty, with more sleep in their eyes, even smellier breath and more internal fluids and waste to be eliminated than normal. Again, this is all good; it's the body doing what it's meant to be doing—cleaning house. If it didn't at least chuck out some of the rubbish every morning, you would be in trouble.

Twenty Four Hour Cleaning Service

The body is a great little cleaning system and, despite what we put in it, will work its liver off to keep things spick-and-span. When you are sleeping, the body repairs itself and eliminates toxins much faster than when you're awake, hence the sweaty armpits and "breath from hell" situation first thing in the morning. However, when you wake up, the body is *still* in the process of having a massive clean up and ideally would like at least a few more hours to continue its work. Unfortunately, we have all been conditioned to eat and drink all kinds of rubbish as soon as we wake up. It has been drummed into us that breakfast is "the most important meal of the day" and that we must load up on "energy foods" before we face the rigors of the day.

Now, I'm not about to say don't eat breakfast; on the contrary, it is very, very important that you get a good breakfast inside you. But as you may have guessed, my idea of what constitutes a good breakfast is very different from what we've all been conditioned to believe we should be eating.

Break Your Fast with Fast Food

The word breakfast is made up of the words *break* and *fast*. During the time you're asleep you are effectively fasting. The time spent sleeping is the longest period you go each day without food or water (unless you're on some kind of mad diet, that is). This means that whatever time you happen to have your first meal is when you *break* your *fast*. Breakfast, however, doesn't have to be in the morning; for some people their first meal is not until the afternoon—but regardless of what time they have their first meal, it's still breakfast. I will, however, be recommending that you do break your fast in the first few hours after you wake up to make sure your sugar levels don't crash to an uncomfortable low. And what better way to break your fast than with some delicious fast food.

Of all the things I teach, getting the right start in the morning is one of the single most important things you can do to restore health and aid weight loss. What you put in your system in the first few hours after waking up is *very*, *very* important for several reasons—so please, listen up.

First, your body is still cleaning house from the day before, and the last thing it needs is someone throwing in difficult-to-digest milk, sugar, syrup, paste, mystery food, and so on while it's trying to clean. It seems almost criminal that we've been taught—by people who really should know better—that things like cereal with cow's milk and a couple of slices of white refined toast with butter is as healthy as pie. The truth is it's a nightmare and will rob your enzyme account like nothing else. It also does nothing to aid the cleaning process. Think about it—how clean would you be if every morning you washed yourself, not with water, but with cream cheese, white paste, and coffee? How groggy would you feel if your all-over shower gel was made of cow glue and maple syrup? So why, oh why, do we expect our insides to stay clean if these are all the tools they have to work with? How on earth is your body ever expected to cleanse itself if that's what it wakes up to? It simply can't. This is why it is very important that for the first five to six hours after you wake the only foods that go into your body are *fast*. You need high water content, nutrient-packed, "predigested by the plant" super foods; foods that help to flush the body of wastes and feed it at the same time. By having these foods in the morning, you not only furnish your system with its first deposit of pure liquid gold, but during this time you don't rob your account either—a total win-win situation.

Secondly, it's much easier to be in full control of your time and demands in the morning than at virtually any other time of the day. It's all too easy to get caught up with other stuff during the day, and there will inevitably be days where you just cannot make a juice later in the day for whatever reason. So make sure you give yourself a fast food kick-start in the morning—you may not get another chance during the day. The strange thing is, you are actually much more likely to eat better and make more juice if you do have a juicy start. The old saying of "start as you mean to carry on" certainly holds water.

Thirdly, what better way to get your "five portions of fruit and veg a day" than having them in one glass and in super-fast, liquid form? One fruit smoothie and boom! Please remember, most people go days without *any* natural food at all, which I must stress again is basically suicide, but just one large glass of liquid sunshine and you're laughing.

Fourthly, the ideal time (although not the *only* time) to have "live" juices is when your stomach is empty. And when are you guaranteed an empty stomach? Yep—in the morning. Fruit is designed to go through the system fast; fruit juice even faster—but it can often struggle if the stomach is like the freeway at 5 pm on a holiday heading out of town. It *ideally* wants a clear run. This is also why I encourage people to have vegetable juice as a starter for lunch or dinner—it gives the juice a chance to leave the stomach before other foods enter, plus it supplies the body with loads of enzymes to help deal with any food that follows. Also, because you've actually "fed" the cells, you eat much less of your main meal because you're genuinely satisfied—pretty neat! This doesn't mean you can't have vegetable juice with a meal; it's simply that the *ideal* time to have it is on an empty stomach. When you wake, your stomach is like the freeway at 3 am Christmas day, and you can be guaranteed the nutrients will get to work—fast.

So with all that in mind it's time to give you the exact recipe for . . .

7

The Juice Master's Fast-Food Breakfast

First Course—WATER

Life as we know it just wouldn't be possible without this stuff—it is an absolute must. During the night, the body works so hard to turn food into usable fuel and chuck out the waste that it becomes pretty dehydrated. It is therefore essential to have clear, nothing-added, cleansing, hydrating liquid entering your system several times a day—*especially* first thing in the morning. So my advice is to have a large glass of cleansing, life-giving water—preferably with slices of fresh lemon or lime in it—first thing in the morning.

Second Course—OXYGEN

Yes oxygen. When I say get some oxygen in you for your second course, I don't mean walk around with a tank on your back, I mean breathe in a way that will really feed and clean your body. The idea behind the Juice Master fast food breakfast is to *feed* your body and cells with everything they need to satisfy your hunger for a good few hours, *without* interfering with the process of elimination. And one thing your body certainly needs when it's hungry is oxygen. There are many people who feel tired and hungry at the end of the day but, instead of eating, they manage to get themselves to the gym. Yet after a workout they come out less tired and not as hungry as when they went in. Why? Because they've supplied their body with what it really needs—oxygen and water. They both help to clean and feed the system.

Just now, millions of liver cells have just died in your body—yes this second. But don't panic, because millions of liver cells have just been created too. Do you know where all the dead cells are? Floating in something called your lymphatic system. You have four times more lymph fluid in your body than you do blood, but, unlike your bloodstream, it doesn't have a pump like the heart and relies on you to deep breathe and move your muscles to help it along. Deep breathing is the single most effective pump for the lymphatic system and will feed your cells and cleanse your system like nothing else. So when you get up in the morning, get into the habit of doing some deep breathing.

Breathe Like a Baby

To get a deep cleanse you need to breathe in a certain way. Most of us don't breathe deeply enough to really oxygenate and clean the system, and when we breathe in, our stomachs tend to go in, when they should in fact go out (watch a baby breathe—they're great at it). Try this breathing exercise to keep the lymph system working effectively. Breathe in (with stomach out) for four counts, hold it for sixteen counts, and slowly let it out for eight counts. Do that at least ten times, four times a day. It doesn't sound like much, but please don't think it's not worth doing, sometimes it's the little things that make a massive difference. This is a very important part of your JM breakfast, as the idea is to supply the body with everything it needs. If you get up and do yoga, go to the gym, have a swim, or such, then this deep breathing exercise is optional, but I must say, I do both.

I also make a point of jumping on my mini-trampoline whenever possible. If you've never had a good bounce (steady!), do yourself a favor and try it. Sticking some good music on your mini-disc and bouncing on your mini-trampoline is perhaps one of the best ways to wake up the body and mind, and what's more – it's FUN (see website for details)!

So now that you've rehydrated your body with cleansing water and given your lymph system a blast of oxygen it's on to the main event.

Main Course—Nutrient-Packed Fast Food

Yep, get up, rehydrate, oxygenate, and get well and truly juiced. And my, oh my, what a choice we have. You can wake up to a tantalizing fruit smoothie such as The Dixie Kicks, The Berry Maguire, or What a Pithy (see pages 166–192 for these and lots of other recipes), or enjoy some liquid sunshine in the form of some creamy, sweet vegetable juices—try the The Enron, The Anne Robin"sun" or The Iron Mike Ty"sun" (see pages 193–217). Each juice and smoothie is packed with life and will not interfere with the cleaning process. Fruit smoothies and juices are super-fab, but vegetable juices are really something you should get into, as most people are far more inclined to eat raw fruit than they are to eat raw veg—and so tend to miss out on all the benefits of raw veg.

All the recipes in the back of this book are simply fab (well I would say that wouldn't I), but there is one that stands out above all the others. It's called The Juice Master Complete (page 194) and contains everything, yep *everything* the body needs to live, not survive—live. Yes, you could live, and I mean really live, on four pints of this veggie smoothie a day . . . if you wanted to. I personally wouldn't want to, I mean imagine going to someone's house for dinner and telling them not to cook for you, as you plan to bring your own super liquid—wouldn't be too long before you're super fit, super healthy and super lonely! However, if you can get into the routine of having one of these babes every morning, you really will be on the fast track to health and vitality. There are, of course, a huge variety of juices and smoothies to choose from, and as you read through the A–Z of fruit and veg and the scrumptious recipes, you will be amazed at the variety.

You may well think that water, oxygen, and juice would never satisfy your morning hunger in a million years, but trust me, do it for a few days and not only will you be super satisfied but anything else will seem completely alien. Conversely, you may be one of those people who just aren't usually hungry in the morning; if so, please do still have the complete JM breakfast (water, air, and fast food). *All* are an essential part of the supreme health programme. Actually, if you aren't usually hungry in the morning this is perfect for you, as you don't have to eat anything—you can drink your breakie.

Don't Panic, You Can Eat Too

If you feel you need to *eat* something in the morning, or if you find you get hungry as the morning progresses, you are more than welcome to have some food. But, as you may have guessed, it must be fast. Whole fruits are the best choice, as they have been predigested by the plant/tree and therefore will not interfere with the cleaning process. Try a few apples, or some fresh blueberries, or a few delicious pears. You can also opt for easy-to-digest veg—an avocado salad, for instance, would be great mid-morning.

As you can see, the JM breakfast is a very important part of what I teach—but I am by no means suggesting that breakfast is the only time to get juiced. Depending on your lifestyle, you can and should juice *any time* of the day or night. In fact, I have some great warm nighttime juices designed to make you sleep like a baby and wake feeling ready to tackle anything (see pages 218–223). Ideally you should be aiming to have two medium glasses of fruit juice/smoothie and two large glasses of vegetable juice whenever possible—and, of course, make some changes to your diet.

The 80 Percent Rule

I haven't got time here to tell you how to completely revise your eating and drinking habits—that's *Slim 4 Life* territory. But to really simplify, the key to incredible health is to ensure that 70–80 percent of what passes your lips daily is high-water-content, as-alive-as-possible fast foods: for example, young leaf spinach and avocado salads, the finest fruits, the most colorful—and of course super-charged—vegetable juices. When you *do* have cooked food, just make sure you have some fruit to start and/or a salad or a creamy, nutrient-packed glass of liquid sunshine with it. That way you will have satisfied your body's need for enzymes and you will not feel inclined to eat as much of the cooked food. It only takes fifteen minutes for liquid fast food to leave the stomach, so, if possible, wait that amount of time before eating your main course. Vegetable juice can also be taken at the same time as a live or cooked meal, something I don't recommend with fruit juices, but please make sure you "chew" your juice. Yes, I did say chew, and no, I haven't gone nuts—

it may be fast food but it's not going to run away!

Big tip—digestion starts in the mouth, so please make a point of "chewing" your juice before you swallow it. Remember, you wouldn't normally eat six carrots, two apples, a stick of celery, half a cucumber, a bunch of spinach, and half an avocado at once, so bear in mind that what you have in your hand is a meal and should be "chewed" (swilled) in the mouth first. This is something you should do with all foods; most people skip the chewing part and wolf down as much as possible, often mentally on the next bite or fork-full before they've even swallowed the first. Take your time with all foods, including juices. They are fairly concentrated and should be drunk *slowly* . . . but not too slowly. It is important to note that once fruit and veg have been broken up and exposed to air they instantly begin to lose some of their life force. Have you ever taken a bite of an apple and left it out? It goes brown. This is called oxidization—or *starting to die,* as I call it. It is therefore essential to **drink your juice as soon as you've made it**.

This point really is important. The sooner you drink your juice after making it, the better. This doesn't mean that if you make a delicious fruit smoothie and have left it in the fridge for many hours that you have to throw it away—it is still full of good carbs, water, and no doubt has a little life left. However, to get the most from your juice you need to "chew" your juice as soon as you make it.

Keeping Your Juice Alive For Longer

Many people want to take a juice with them to work to have later in the day, so here's a handy tip. Get an empty flask and put it in the freezer with the lid off. Next morning, make your juice, pour into the flask, and seal with the lid *immediately*. That way the ice-cold temperature and sealed unit of the flask will keep your juice "alive" for much longer. The "life span" of juice is largely dependent on the machine you use (as you will read later in "What Machine?"), but if you are going to store your juice, regardless of what machine the above tip is the best method. Just make sure that you add some lemon or lime juice to your juice (fruit or veg) to slow down deterioration. Have you noticed how quickly an avocado goes black when it's exposed to air? And how it stays fresher longer with a touch of lemon juice? You just can't beat the beauty of nature.

If you think this is all too daunting for whatever reason and the thought of not having your bagels, toast, cereal, bacon, or eggs is just too much to even contemplate, please *still* have a glass of freshly extracted liquid gold in the morning—and have it half an hour before your usual breakfast. Just try it, and meanwhile get hold of a copy of *Slim 4 Life*—it will help you really get to grips with your diet and make the change.

The *Super-Fast* Track to a Slim, Energy-Driven Body

If you want to really clear and clean your system and put it on the fast track to health, then a "spring clean" is great. The following program is without question the fastest way to cleanse your system of built-up rubbish without having to go to the somewhat drastic action of having someone shove a pipe up your bottom to suck it all out! However, a spring clean isn't just for those of us who feel unhealthy and desperately in need of one, we all need a helping hand now and then. No matter how "healthy" or "clean" we think we are, virtually everyone could do with one of these about four times a year. Ladies and gentlemen I present . . .

8

The Juice Master's Ultimate Spring Cleaning Plan

The following eating plan is a *suggestion* and will not be for everyone, but if you manage to get into the right frame of mind where you're as happy as organic pie to follow it, the rewards are quite simply remarkable. I suggest that you follow the plan once every three months. The juicing/eating plan I have outlined so far in the book will give you truly remarkable health. There's just no question your hair will shine, your eyes will sparkle, you'll lose excess weight if you need to, you'll tap into a level of energy you haven't had in years, your nails will be stronger, you'll be calmer, and your thinking will become razor sharp—not bad rewards I'd say. The following eating plan will provide all these benefits—only in a much faster time frame.

The chances are you have a massive buildup of rubbish in your digestive system and clearly some of the nutrients, even in juice, will not be able to get through to do their job. So in order to give your fast food the fast track it needs, you need to begin the plan with a mini fast.

DAYS ONE AND TWO
The Two-Day Water and Lemon/Lime Cleanse

Yes that means you should have *nothing* else for two days, just water. Each day have at least five quarts of water with slices of lemon and lime in it. Hot water with a few chunks of lemon or lime is particularly good —especially first thing in the morning and last thing at night. Whenever you feel hungry have some water—don't forget to carry some with you if you need to go out. I also want you to do the breathing exercise (see page 57), as this is an important part of the cleansing process. Make sure you rest as much as possible and sleep, sleep, sleep. It sounds difficult to go without food for two days—but it is only two days and it is for your benefit. If this really is too daunting, you can do one day and then continue as follows.

DAY THREE
Drink Only Water and Vegetable Juice

On day three you need to have at least three quarts of water, again with lemon and/or lime slices. You should also have two to three pints of vegetable juice—try "The Hoover" (page 202), The Hawny Juice (page 196) and The Iron Mike Ty"sun" (page 204). Remember to drink your juice slowly. Don't forget to do your breathing exercises.

DAYS FOUR AND FIVE
Water, Organic Apples, and the JM Complete

During days four and five you can eat—hooray! Hang on; don't get too excited, I haven't finished. You can eat . . . organic apples. Other than that you need to drink at least three quarts of water with lemon and/or lime (as you can see the water's pretty important) and have three pints of my ultimate vegetable smoothie, The Juice Master Complete (see page 194). Once again, drink plenty of either hot or cold lemon/lime water when you first wake up and just before you go to bed—and remember to do the breathing exercises.

DAYS SIX AND SEVEN
Two Natural Days

This is where I actively encourage you to eat, but, as you've been cleansing, the last thing you want to do is load your system with processed food. For days six and seven you may eat and drink as much as you like, but make sure it's "live" and natural. The only fruits I encourage on these days are apples and berries (of any kind), but no fruit juices or smoothies. Make sure you have your three quarts of lemon/lime water and do your deep breathing. Have a few creamy vegetable juices (see recipe chapter), one of which should be a Juice Master Complete. Make a point of having at least one large avocado salad with lemon/lime juice as a dressing.

Even when you're not following the cleansing plan, I would encourage you to have a "natural" day once a week, every week—it really does make a huge difference to your energy and lifespan.

DAYS EIGHT TO TWENTY-ONE
Easy on the Man-Made Carbs and Skip the Wheat and Yeast

This period is all about consolidation, so I want you to avoid a few things that are hard work for the body. I'm not a "no-carbohydrate" guy (well obviously not, 'cause *all* fruits and vegetables are a source of carbohydrate) and I really hate these high-protein diets that seem to be all the rage at the moment. However, that doesn't mean I'm a fan of "man-made" carbohydrates such as bread, pasta, white rice and so on. These products have caused more problems than they've solved over the years, and there's a huge chance that you will have some problems relating to these foods. The main problem is the white refined ones, which I encourage you to NEVER go near, but just to complete the clean, go easy on *all* man-made carbs from days eight to twenty-one.

I'm not saying *don't* eat them, just make sure that only your **lunchtime meal** contains *whole-grain*, man-made carbohydrates. In fact, a rule not just for this 21-day, plan but also beyond if you are trying to lose weight, is to adhere to a 6pm Carb Boycott. This means no man-made carbs after 6pm. This rule alone can produce some pretty amazing results on the weight-loss front. Make sure that any lunchtime bread or pasta you buy is yeast/wheat free—look for rye, pumpernickel, spelt, and so on. Whole-grain rice is about your best bet, with some delicious stir-fried veg and a frothy glass of liquid gold. Also skip the fruit smoothies and juices and EAT your fruit instead (for reasons I'll come to in just a sec).

So for days eight to twenty-one, eat as much fruit as you like, drink plenty of water and vegetable juices, have plenty of delicious salads and soups, and some cold-water fish like sardines, mackerel, and salmon (and, if you like, some organic white meat)—and enjoy!

Each and every day on the ultimate cleanse you will look and feel better than ever, and one thing is for sure, by the time you reach the end, your energy level will have rocketed. If you are doing this to lose some weight as well as to be healthy and radiant, I can also guarantee a significant loss of excess weight. In fact, if you don't lose a chunk of weight after doing this I'll eat my piano!

If you've now read through the plan and feel inclined to give it a go, do read the following warning first.

WARNING

Have you noticed that when you are having a real mother of a clean in your house that it looks ten times worse before it looks better? This is what happens when you open the cupboards and start clearing out the mess. Your body is the same. When you "clean house" it is not unusual during the first few days to get headaches, feel tired, have disrupted sleeping patterns, and basically feel like you are dead on your feet. Some people also experience emotional changes. These are all good signs, although they might not feel like it, and are just part of the process of getting rid of toxins.

You will not automatically get these side effects—many people feel good from the start. However, it's best to be aware of them.

(If you feel this kind of plan would prove too tricky in your environment, look out for Juice Master Weeks and weekends away—see author's page for contact details.)

There's just one more topic I need to cover before we get on to the practical stuff. There has been, how can I put it, a heated debate about sugar in general over the past few years, but there is one particular sugar some people seem to have got slightly confused about—fruit sugar. Such has been the confusion that we now have some people believing that eggs and bacon swimming around in saturated fat is better for you than an apple (thanks, Dr. Atkins and co., we just love you!). However, there is no denying that once fruit is *juiced* or dried the sugars can, if you don't follow certain guidelines, cause problems. The guidance is simple really, eating fruit is fine but . . .

9

Don't Overdo the Fruit Juice

Eating fruit really doesn't pose a problem. Whole fruit contains loads of fiber that helps to prevent the fruit sugars entering the bloodstream too rapidly and sending your sugar levels sky high. When you extract the juice from fruit, however, it's missing the fiber and so has the *potential* to raise sugar levels rapidly. This doesn't mean for one second that you shouldn't have "live" fruit juices, and it doesn't mean they are like white refined sugar and bad for you—they're not. Fruit juice contains over 90 percent of the nutrients of the whole fruit, so it's brimming with goodness and will do you a world of good. Let me make that quite clear . . . FRUIT JUICES AND SMOOTHIES *ARE* GOOD FOR YOU. The last thing I want to do is put you off fruit juice—you just need to be aware of a few guidelines. So with that in mind, here's my guide to a happy fruitful life:

1. Always "chew" your juice (i.e. "swill" round in your mouth) and *take your time* drinking it.
2. Where possible, have a fruit smoothie as opposed to juice (see the Q & A, page 246), as the fibers from the whole fruits will help to slow down the absorption of sugars into the bloodstream.
3. Add water and ice to "thin" the juice.
4. Have no more than two to four medium glasses of fruit juice a day.*

For many people, a fruit juice or fruit smoothie with a little ice drunk *slowly* (very important that) will pose no problem whatsoever; on the contrary, it will have you oozing with vitality before you can say gooseberry.

However, a lot of people *do* have sugar problems due to years of eating the wrong kinds of sugars. Therefore, if you are diabetic,* suffer from candida, have athlete's foot or thrush, or are already suffering from low blood sugar and/or have a weight problem, make your fruit juice with about half mineral water. That way there is no danger of loading your bloodstream with too much natural sugar. Also, have smoothies, as *whole* fruits blended, rather than just juiced, slow down the rate at which sugars are released into the bloodstream. Another good tip is to add some nuts, such as natural almonds, to the blender, as this also helps to prevent rapid absorption of concentrated fruit sugars into the bloodstream. Now I'm not a fan of dairy products, as you know, but for people with any of the above problems I recommend you mix some live goat's yogurt in with your smoothie. Goats, like us, have one stomach (cows have four), so not only is their milk easier for us to digest, but live goat's yogurt has loads of "friendly bacteria" that help to curb an overgrowth of candida in the gut. Yogurt also helps to slow down the rapid absorption of fruit sugars into the bloodstream. If you're a vegan, please don't think for one second this is a must—it's just one of many ways to prevent sugar surges. Better still—and for *best* results with candida, diabetes, and excess weight—during the first month *at least*, make a point, where possible, of . . .

* If you are diabetic and in any doubt make sure you *always* consult your doctor first.

Eating Your Fruit and *Drinking* Your Veg

Clearly that doesn't mean don't *eat* veg, it just means when it comes to "live" liquid you should go for vegetable not fruit juices—fruit should be *eaten*. Please understand this doesn't mean you can never have fruit juices or smoothies, it is simply that if you suffer from any of the above-mentioned problems, your pancreas is going to need a few weeks or months to repair—essential if you have a candida/weight problem. If you do have fruit juices or smoothies during the first month, please *always* follow the guidelines outlined above.

Contrary to what you may imagine, drinking a vegetable juice for breakfast is just as enjoyable as a having a fruit juice. Made in the right way, a vegetable juice is pure taste and health heaven—no matter what the time of day. The base that I use for most of my vegetable juices includes apple, but this is fine, as apple juice does not cause excess sugar problems. Once again though, take your time with it—it is a meal. There's no need to add water or ice to your vegetable juices if you keep your veg chilled; juicing them straight from the fridge means you'll instantly have a cool and refreshing veg juice.

Most people, however, *do* opt for the fruit versions to break their fast in the mornings, as I used to and occasionally still do (well they are super lovely), but the sooner you get your taste buds in training and start enjoying the pure liquid magic that is veg juice, the better. Drinking rich, creamy, sweet-tasting vegetable juice in the morning and *eating* some organic apples to go along with it will have you radiant and healthy in no time. Again when you *eat* fruit (except hybrid, mass-produced bananas) there is little danger of loading the bloodstream with too much sugar. It's only if you drink loads of it *undiluted* and *very fast* that you can possibly experience problems.

So is that it, Mr. Juice Master—can I get cracking now? Yes indeedy, don't see why not, you should be about as mentally prepared as possible, and you should, if you've really taken this stuff on board, be chomping at the bit itching to get juiced. But before you just go off and buy the first machine you see or rub the dust off your old one, you need to know how to make juicing as easy as possible and a part of your daily life. The biggest argument that people put forward against juicing is that it takes a long time and that cleaning the machine is a real pain in the butt. However, if you're prepared, it can be super fast. Before I present you with my twelve-step "followship" for making your juice super fast, you're going to need to make some changes to your kitchen. No, don't panic, no need to get the builders in, you just need to know exactly . . .

10

How to Set up a Juice Master Fast-Food Kitchen

 Let me ask you a question—where do you put your cooker when you've finished using it? What about your sink? How about your washing machine? Don't worry, I haven't completely lost the plot, I do realize these sound like barmy questions, yet if I asked the same question about a juicing machine and blender it would sound perfectly reasonable. Why? Because with your cooker, sink, washing machine, and so on you *expect* to use them all the time and so want easy access to them. However, juicing is often seen as something you do every now and again, so most people who own a juicer keep it hidden away in a cupboard or, if it has managed to get residency on the worktop, it will usually be fenced in with all kinds of rubbish, making its actual use virtually impossible. This inevitably leads to people thinking juicing is a right royal pain in the proverbial and just not worth the hassle. In reality, however, when you know how to do it, making a juice should take five to fifteen minutes max, and that *includes* cleaning time.

Out of Sight Out of Mind

If you want to make juicing a *daily* part of your life, then the first thing you need to do is give your juice extractor pride of place in your kitchen. If space is tight, make room by shifting your nutrient destroyer, sorry, I mean microwave, into the cupboard instead of the juicer. Better still—sell your microwave! A microwave does for food and health what Ken Lay did for the stock market. The truth is unless you have *easy* access to your juicer you won't use it—"out of site out of mind" as they say, so find a permanent worktop home for your new best friend. (We'll look at the choice of machines on page 76, so don't worry, I will point you in the right direction.)

Size Matters When You Get a Board

Something else that should have a prominent place in your kitchen is a good, *large* chopping board. Unlike a juicer, most people not only own one of these but have usually already given it worktop space. If you haven't already got one, or you have a very small excuse for one, then it's time to invest. What you need is the *largest* wooden, square chopping board that will fit comfortably on your worktop. As silly as it may sound, the right chopping board could make or break your decision to juice on any particular day. Remember the key to *daily* juicing is speed and simplicity—if you can't fit all your fruits or veg on your chopping board, have difficulty cutting them due to lack of space, and find yourself with nowhere to put your titbits, then there's a good chance you will throw in the juice towel. So a good, large chopping board is an *essential* part of your juice station and should be placed close to your juicer.

Pack the Knife

Another absolute must is a *very* sharp, good-quality, *self-sharpening* knife. A blunt knife will slowly but surely dissolve your enthusiasm and eat away at your zest for making freshly extracted juice. The main knife I use cost about eighteen dollars—to some people that's a lot for a knife and to others it's a little. When I first bought it, I fell into the "a lot" category but as it's been with me for six years so far and hasn't needed sharpening once, I now see in reality it falls into the "bloody good value" category. If you haven't got ten to twenty dollars for a good self-sharpening knife, simply use some of the leftover cash from selling your microwave! A sharp knife is even more important than a good sized chopping board, so get hold of the best knife you can afford.

With Nail Brush and I

To make cleaning quick and simple you will again need the right tools for the job. Now most juicing machines you buy come with their own cleaning brush/es designed specifically for cleaning the mesh filter part of the juicer, which you will find on all machines. Most parts of a juice machine can simply be placed under a warm tap and boom—they're clean. The mesh filter, which acts just like a colander/sieve stopping the pulp but allowing the juice to flow, is the part which inevitably requires slightly more attention when cleaning than the other parts and is where the nail brush is needed—without it you will struggle, so for the sake of fifty cents—get one!

Read All about It

Here's an excellent tip for your fast food kitchen; just before you make a juice, place a few large sheets of old newspaper under your chopping board and juicing machine—enough to cover the whole area. Then after you have finished juicing and you take apart your machine, you can simply scoop out all the waste and place it on the paper. Any peel or bits on the chopping board also just scrape off onto the paper. You then simply put the machine parts and chopping board in the sink, wrap all the leftovers in the paper, and chuck them into the garbage. You are then left with a clean surface, no wiping needed! So keep a drawer spare for your old papers—they are a godsend for speeding up cleaning.

On the Go? Get a Flask

An absolute must when it comes to regular juicing is a "bullet" flask. This wonderful piece of kitchen/outdoor kit means you can make a "juice to go" (see Juice Master Juicing Tips, page 85). I recommend the silver bullet types; you know, the ones you find in camping shops. They don't have a handle and look like a large bullet. These are great for sticking in your freezer. If you only have the big-handled type, that's fine for the job—it's just a bit cumbersome to carry around.

Don't Put It on the Plastic—Put It in It!

Here's another superb tool to help make cleaning super fast—plastic bags. Virtually all centrifugal juicers have a "pulp container" somewhere on the machine—usually at the back. Its job is pretty self-explanatory—to collect the left over pulp or "waste". This is often an extra part to clean, but place a plastic bag (size to match the container on your machine) inside the pulp container just before you juice and all you need do is lift it out and chuck it in the garbage. Better still, if you have a garden or window box, empty the pulp into the soil—plants and wildlife love it.

Hey Big Blender!

One final thing you will need to complete your fast-food juice kitchen is a decent blender. Blenders are an invaluable part of your kitchen. They are not just brilliant for making smoothies, but are great for making guacamole and beautiful soups. There are many, many blenders on the market, and in the chapter "What Machine?" I will run through the ones that get Juice Master approval along, of course, with the right juicer for you.

Before then you need to know the key behind successful regular juicing; it's no good having a juice kitchen without knowing how to use it—yep making a juice may be easy, but you need to know exactly how to make it *correctly*, more importantly you need to know . . .

11

How to Make a Juice— Fast

The Twelve-Step "Followship"

The biggest complaint I hear when it comes to juicing is the time it takes to make a juice and clean the machine. But think about it, given that your health is the single most important thing in the world to you and your family and affects every aspect of your life, it shouldn't matter a jot if you had to get up an hour earlier to feed your cells. However, the good news is that the "it takes an eternity brigade" have got it wrong—juicing and cleaning can be super fast, but you need to know how to go about it. Here are the twelve simple steps to juicing success—

1. Get all the ingredients you need on your chopping board before you do anything else.
2. Prepare, wash and cut to size the produce you need for your juice and put back the rest.
3. Half fill sink with warm water and dish washing liquid.
4. Turn on machine and juice everything in one go.
5. Put jug of juice to one side and begin cleaning.
6. Scrape bits off chopping board onto newspaper and wash board immediately.

7. Undo machine and lift out any pulp in nooks and crannies and place on paper.
8. Put all parts of machine (except electric base) into the sink of warm water.
9. Fold newspaper and throw in garbage or empty contents in garden and paper in bin.
10. Run tap with warm water and keep it running.
11. Most pieces of the machine can be cleaned by simply rinsing them under the tap. The mesh part will need the nail brush and tap treatment.
12. Quickly run a dish towel over machine, put back together, and leave everything in a position where it's once again inviting and easy to juice.

Before we crack on to the next section, I just want to reiterate one very, very important point from the twelve steps: when it comes to regular juicing make certain you . . .

ALWAYS CLEAN THE MACHINES IMMEDIATELY AFTER USING THEM

It takes a few minutes to clean a machine that's just been used, but leave it a while and you'll be at it a looooong time. Also, even if it has a "you can clean it in the dishwasher" label on your machine—don't. It tends to discolour the machine and in reality isn't that practical. If you come home to a dirty juicer in your dishwasher there is just no way you'll either wait for the cycle to finish to make some, or get it out and clean it. It will be in there until you find a load of other stuff to clean. Trust me; after you make your juice just clean the blooming thing in the sink.

Now of course you're going to need a machine to clean and the most commonly asked question is . . .

12

What Machine?

Trying to choose a machine is a pretty confusing business. There are many different types, many individual needs, and many different budgets, so there's no single machine that will suit everyone. However, to make life easier I've broken the choice down into three individual categories—bronze, silver, and gold.

BRONZE MEDAL MACHINES

Don't be put off by a "bronze" medal machine—just because it "only" has a Juice Master bronze medal label doesn't mean it's not a truly splendid machine or that it's not worth buying—far from it. For any machine to get Juice Master approval it *must* be good. There are many, many juice extractors out there that don't come close to making the JM bronze grade, and if the machine I suggest in this category meets your needs and budget then this so-called bronze machine could, as far as you're concerned, be gold.

Most people start off with a bronze medal juicer and, to be fair, I advise that they do—it usually does them proud for many, many years. However, to get Juice Master bronze medal approval it needs to be much more than a simple "starter juicer"—it needs to fulfil the following criteria:

- Be able to extract juice from fruit and veg with ease
- Have a fairly large chute to feed in whole fruits and veg without too much cutting
- Possess a good motor that lasts
- Be easy to clean
- Look good
- Cost under sixty dollars

CENTRIFUGAL—NOW THERE'S A WORD!

The bronze medal machine I recommend is a centrifugal juicer. You will hear the word "centrifugal" a lot in the juicing world, so it's worth an explanation. This type of juicer chops your fruit and veg into small pieces and then throws them against a spinning bowl that in turn separates the juice from the fiber. Centrifugal juicers are often slammed by certain juicing/health experts who say that the high speed of the machine heats the produce, leaving it nutritionally inferior to what you get from what's known as a "masticating" juicer (I'll come to those in a second). What they're saying is correct, but that doesn't mean the juice you get is nutritionally dead—far from it. The juice you get from a bronze medal centrifugal machine still contains *plenty* of "live" juicy nutrients, all of which are fan-dab-ie-dose-ie for your mental and physical health.

Centrifugal machines are, on the whole, much quicker and easier to use and certainly a whole heap cheaper than masticating ones. So if time as well as money is short, you are actually better off with a centrifugal machine, as you're more likely to use it regularly. And you're better off getting loads of *slightly* inferior juice *daily* than small amounts of the best quality juice occasionally. All you need to remember when using a centrifugal machine is that you need to drink the juice *immediately* (or as close as) after making it as the heat generated by the machine means the juice does "die" faster. (There is a way to keep juice for longer without losing too many nutrients and this is covered in the "Juice Master Juicing Tips" on page 85.)

Another cry from "experts" not keen on this type of machine is that it doesn't extract sufficient juice from the fibers and leaves the pulp too wet. While this is true, it's not the end of the world—it simply means you use *slightly* more produce. If you are worried about some goodness being left in the pulp, it's worth knowing that in tests with *good* centrifugal juicers 90 per cent of the nutrients remain in the juice.

Now where was I? Oh that's right, bronze medal juicers. At the moment, there's only one which really makes The Juice Master grade—Ladies and Gentlemen I give you . . .

The Juice Master Junior
by Moulinex Krups

Well I don't actually give you, you have to invest—but my, what an investment this little space-age looking machine is. What's more, compared to its much lesser rivals in the starter juicer market, it's an absolute bargain.

In the U.K., Moulinex used to have a slogan:
"Moulinex makes things simple and that includes the price"

Well that slogan still holds very true. The Juice Master Junior is Moulinex's newest model, and its design, motor, and juicing capabilities are simply the best *by far* in the starter juicer bracket. I still have no idea how they put together such an incredible machine for so little money. Unfortunately, you can't buy this model in the U.S., but it is available on the website. With shipping charges, this would work out as too much, but there are other machines in the U.S. that are pretty good in this price range. Hopefully the JM Junior will be on sale in the U.S. soon, please check the website for details. If I sound pretty impressed by this machine, it's because I am. My first ever juicer was the Moulinex 753P1, a machine whose motor simply refused to burn out (unusual for a starter machine). They discontinued the 753P1 some time ago and during that time there hasn't been a starter machine that I felt I could recommend—until now. I've put this little beauty through its paces and it can make three pints of juice without having to take it apart "mid-juice", which is brilliant. The JM Junior also has a larger pulp container than the 753, has a more powerful motor and extracts the pulp more efficiently.

I do realize that you can get other starter machines cheaper—and some just a little more expensive—but I assure you I wouldn't put my name to any of them, and they just aren't good value. Most are very small and so blooming difficult and tedious to use that you're likely to give up after about a week.

So that's the starter juicer taken care of—The Juice Master Junior by Moulinex. This bronze beauty will keep you happily juicing for a long time to come. However, if you already know that juicing will be a way of life for you and your family for years to come then you may well want to go straight for silver.

HIGH HO SILVER!

Strictly speaking this next machine should have a gold label, but gold is reserved for a "masticating" juice extractor (all will be explained soon). However, when it comes to centrifugal juicers—which, I will repeat, are the most common and easy to use—this next machine is gold medal stuff. In fact, I would even go as far as to say in my humble opinion it is . . .

The Best Semi-Pro Centrifugal Juicing Machine in the World

A bold statement, but I believe it's an accurate one. To get that kind of JM seal of approval it has to be good—bloody good in fact, and **The Juice Master Deluxe** really is that good. I was so impressed, I couldn't buy the company like the great Victor Kiam, but I put my name to it. Those of you who know me of old will be aware that for years I refused to put my name on any juice extractor, as I knew they could always be improved upon and that it would only be a matter of time. Well that time has arrived and I honestly believe this machine has everything you need and more . . .

Two-speed, long-lasting motor—This is an excellent feature. The lower the speed at which you extract your juice, the more "live" nutrients it retains. This is why I recommend whenever possible using the slower speed for green leafy veg, cucumber, celery, and such and whacking it up to top speed for hard fruits and veg like carrots, pears, and apples. The high-powered motor has also been built with *daily* usage in mind, so is not about to burn up after a few months like some on the market.

Very large pulp container—This feature is a must, especially if you have a large family or need to make juice for many people. A large container at the back of the machine to collect the pulp means you can make several pints of juice before having to empty it. There's nothing worse than having to take the machine apart when you're in the middle of making a juice.

Large feeder—One of the complaints about juicing has been the time it takes to chop up fruit and veg to fit through the feeder. Well, this beauty has a very large chute that has the capacity to take three whole apples at once—priceless.

See-through lid—This is an amazingly simple but essential feature for this kind of semi-pro machine. The see-through lid lets you see what's going on as you juice, which means if it does get clogged you can see the problem instantly.

Stainless steel *self-sharpening* cutting basket—Apart from the motor, this is one part of the machine that will see more action than any other, so it needs to be built to do the job—and this one certainly has been.

It's round—A round, curvy machine is quick and easy to clean.

Once again, do not be put off by the fact that I've given The Juice Master Deluxe a silver medal. It is undoubtedly the reigning champion of centrifugal juicers and worthy of gold status within that category. This machine will retail at around $175, but really is well worth the money. It has a large chute that takes whole apples, is quiet as a mouse, is easy to clean, and extracts more juice than most other centrifugal juicers. All this means it receives the Juice Master silver medal approval. The only down side is that it won't actually be available until 2004. Until then, dust off your old machine, get yourself a JM Junior, or look for other good silver medal machines on my Website.

GOING FOR GOLD

The only reason the following machines have been given a Juice Master gold rating is because they are what's known as masticating juicers. This means that instead of chopping the produce and throwing it against a spinning bowl to separate the juice from the fiber, it grinds the produce into very small particles and presses them through a screen. These machines cost a great deal more than centrifugal juicers and unless you are very serious about juicing and have some spare cash, I certainly wouldn't kick off my juicing life with one of these machines. However, if you do have the money and the time (they do take longer than centrifugal juicers) and are looking to get a gold machine to complement your bronze or silver, then they are a very good long-term investment.

The additional cost is justified for many reasons. Firstly most masticating juicers do so much more than simply make juice. You can also make nut and seed spreads, dairy-free "ice cream" and baby foods. Because the juice is extracted at much lower speeds than a centrifugal juicer, more of the "live" enzymes stay intact, and due to the way in which it presses, they also tend to extract more juice from produce. In addition, the motors in these machines just never seem to die—and when I say never I mean NEVER—and most come with at least a five-year guarantee.

The Green Star 1000

There are many of these masticating machines on the market, but again not all make the Juice Master grade. There are, however, two that stand out more than the others and therefore get the JM gold grading. The first is the Green Star 1000, which retails at anything from $400–$500 (well, gold is expensive). This is the only juice extractor I know of that has something called a twin-gear magnetic system (sounds funky!). What this means is that it extracts the juice in a way that prevents the juice from oxidizing and losing vital vitamins and minerals. This means you can store the juice you make from this beauty for two whole days, keeping most of its life force intact. If you ever do use this machine you will notice that the "pulp" is bone dry after making juice, meaning you have extracted just about all the juice that can be had from the produce. This, in the long run, saves money.

The Champion of Champions

Another machine that I just have to mention is Champion. This baby has been highly recommended for many, many years by just about anyone who knows anything about juicing. Once again it's a masticating machine and has a JM gold medal seal of approval. It's slightly cheaper than the Green Star 1000 (but still has a five-year guarantee), but is actually more versatile, as it juices fruits with ease. It cannot, however, do wheatgrass and the like, and it extracts the juice at a slightly higher RPM, meaning you cannot store the juice for as long as juice from the Green Star. To be fair, it's hard to choose between these two gold beauties. If you are into either eating or blending your fruits for fab smoothies and therefore only really need a machine designed with veg and green leafy plant matter in mind, then the Green Star is your best bet. If, on the other hand, you want a "gold" machine that will do the lot (except wheatgrass etc.) then go for the Champion.

Many juice or raw food "experts" would say the best juicing machine in the world is the Norwalk, named after the great Dr. Norman Walker. However, it costs $2000 (which for the vast majority of people is out right away), it takes forever to get a glass of juice from it and an evening to clean! In contrast, all the machines that get the JM seal of approval are spookily quick at producing juice and are easy to clean (especially if you use the twelve simple steps).

I personally have bronze, silver, and gold in my kitchen, but then I am "The Juice Master"! I have The Juice Master Junior, a silver medal machine, and a masticating machine. I tend to use my JM Junior for a quick and easy juice on the go, the Silver Juicer if I'm making loads for many people, and the Green Star 1000 or Champion for dairy-free ice-creams and creamy veg juices, if I have more time. For most people, I'd recommend kicking off with The Juice Master Junior—you can always upgrade if you find your needs become greater.

Now that we've sorted you out with a juicer we need to look at blenders. Yep, a juice kitchen just isn't complete without one of these life-savers and, once again, as there are just so many on the market, I've put them into the JM bronze, silver, and gold categories.

Very "Handy" Bronze Blender

Now I must say I don't usually recommend that people get a bronze medal blender as they are the hand-held types, but if that's all your budget allows, then to kick things off it's certainly better than a clip round the ear with a wet kipper. Actually, hand blenders can be really good and you can do almost the same with these as with a jug-type "silver medal" version. Just to clarify, a hand-blender is just that—a blender you hold in your hand. They usually come with a blending beaker; the idea being that you put your fruits, nuts, whatever into the long beaker, add a little juice, water, or ice and blend away. The main problem with this type of machine is that the beaker they come with does tend to be a little small and so I highly recommend using a larger jug (no need to buy one you've probably got loads in your cupboard). They can also be a bit messy compared to the silver or gold versions. There are several "handy" blenders on the market all ranging in price and ability.

Silver

In all likelihood you've probably got a silver medal blender somewhere in your kitchen, either as part of a food processor or on its own. A silver medal blender is the "jug" type; you know, like the ones you see at bars. They usually have a plastic see-through jug and "click on" and "click off" the base. To qualify for the JM silver medal seal of approval the blender has to be able to do ice and frozen fruits with ease and must have a large jug. There are many on the market and you shouldn't have a problem picking one up for about $40. Just make sure the one you buy can do ice and has a large jug and a good, long-lasting motor.

Gold

To qualify for gold medal status a blender doesn't actually need a lot—
a *glass* jug usually does the trick. One downside to the silver medal
machines, if any, is that the plastic jug gets worn after a while, whereas a
glass jug doesn't. Glass pretty much lasts as long as you do. The motor on
glass-jugged machines tends to be better too, but then the cost is always
higher. Most people kick off with a silver medal blender and it lasts them
for years. But if you do have the money, a gold machine not only has a
better motor, looks better, and has a jug that will never fade, but on the
whole they do tend to blend better.

WHERE CAN YOU GET THEM?

All machines mentioned here are available from my Website
www.thejuicemaster.com. Machines are usually dispatched same day. If
you prefer to get them in store, please check out the Website for outlets.
You can call us too on 011 44 0845 1 30 28 29.

LET'S GET CRACKING . . . ALMOST!

So now you know why you should juice, how to juice, and what
machines you need to do the job. All you need now is a complete guide
to all the fruits and vegetables I recommend for juicing, some gorgeous
recipes, and a bit of a Q & A session at the end. Please make a point
of reading about *each* fruit and vegetable—you'll find yourself saying,
"well put me on a metal tray and slide me down a hill, I never knew
that!" (well maybe). It also provides guidance on preparing fruit and veg
ready for juicing or smoothie-ing (if there is such a word). Oh one more
thing . . . when you find that you have exhausted the recipes in this
book, feel free to make up your own. With a few basic rules and a bit of
imagination, anyone—yep, even *you*—can become a master of the juice.
So before we move on to the A–Z of fruit and veg here's . . .

13

The Juice Master's Juicing Tips

1. **Use a crapple base** On the whole, fruit and vegetable juices don't mix well. Like everything in life though, there are exceptions. Limes, lemons, apples, and pineapples mix ok with vegetable juices—hooray! Trust me, without these exceptions vegetable juice would be about as appealing as dinner with Hannibal Lecter. To ensure that your vegetable juice tastes wonderful every time, make sure one-half to three-fourths of your juice is made up of apple, carrot, or tomato juice, or a combination of these. Personally I'm not a fan of tomato juice (if you have psoriasis please never have tomato juice, or tomatoes), so I either have a pure carrot juice base (nice and sweet) or more commonly a mixture of carrot and apple (commonly known as crapple). You will see in the recipe section a lot of my veg juices have a crapple base. This doesn't mean that if you mixed orange juice with, say, carrot that your head would explode! It just means, other than the exceptions I've outlined, vegetable juice and fruit juices don't mix very well.

2. **Never juice leeks or onion and go easy on the garlic** I do include some garlic with the Dr. Juice recipes (garlic is explained in full on page 153) but leek and onion really suck, even when mixed with other juices.

3. **Green juices are very potent as is raw beetroot—so don't drink them alone** I don't mean don't drink them by *your*self, I mean by *them*selves. Always mix with other juices such as carrot, apple, pineapple, etc. A large handful of spinach makes a small amount of juice, but it's very powerful and will turn all of your juice green; beetroot is even more potent and the small amount of juice you get from one small beetroot will turn a green juice very red indeed. The only exceptions are cucumber and celery.

4. **Always clean the machine after use** Yes I've mentioned it before, but it's blooming important.

5. **Make a smoothie—super fast** Sometimes you will be in such a hurry that you won't have time to juice. If so, there is a way to make a super-fast smoothie without even touching your juicer. Simply chuck some fresh/frozen fruits into the blender, for instance berries, banana, kiwi, passion, even some live goat's yogurt, add a large handful of ice, blend, and enjoy. If you don't use yogurt and find it's too thick or not blending well, simply add some cold mineral water.

6. **Add a little spice to your juice** Make no mistake, fresh juices taste fab, but every now and then you can spice them up. I often add cinnamon power to fruit juices and smoothies, and nutmeg and ginger to vegetable juices.

7. **Freeze what you don't use** You may find you over-buy produce and much of what you buy goes bad. If anything is on the turn simply chop it up and freeze it. Unlike cooking, when you freeze "live" produce you only lose about 5 percent of the enzymes. When freezing bananas, please make sure you peel them first. You can also make a juice at night, put it in a flask, and freeze it. You can then take the flask to work and let the juice slowly defrost.

8. **Juicing can be cheap** People will often argue that juicing is expensive, that you have to use a lot of produce to get a juice.

Firstly, "what price health?" Secondly, this often isn't true, as it depends on what machine you use. Not only that, but when you juice you can pick up some real bargains. Often the market stalls or greengrocers sell fruit and veg that are just "on the turn" for next to nothing. You would never eat it in a day, but you can make a good load of juice out of it and simply chop and freeze the rest. Clearly though, fresh organic produce is best, so you don't want to do this all the time.

9. **Wash your produce but don't peel it** The majority of nutrients in fruit and veg are to be found just beneath the skin. Obviously this tip doesn't apply to bananas or oranges.

10. **Feed the pulp to your garden** If you have time, put the leftover pulp in the garden—'tis the best compost in the world.

11. **Experiment** Feel free to experiment, don't just stick to other people's recipes. There are literally thousands of fruits and vegetables out there, make your own blend and name it after yourself.

12. **Put some music on while you juice** No I'm not a groove short of a full disc! When you get up and get juiced have a blast of your favorite music—it will help juice you for the day. Don't knock it till you've tried it.

13. **Go green whenever you can** Yep, whenever possible get those green leafy veg down ya. They are the main key to unlocking your health and vitality—pure liquid sunshine to your cells. If you've got a garden—even a windowbox—try growing your own. You won't find anything fresher or more satisfying than creating juice from something you've grown.

14. **Never eat processed food two to three hours before you sleep and *always* have a large glass of water just before bed** This has got nothing to do with juicing but is part of "you do

need to know" stuff. If you cat cooked food before you sleep, you will certainly wake up with a degree of junk food hangover syndrome. If you feel hungry at night, make fruit the snack, or a salad, maybe some nuts, or a "night night" juice (see page 218), but please make a point of skipping the processed muck and furnishing your cells with a glass of clear cool refreshing water.

15. **Get a Juice Master wall-chart** How's that for an ad! The reason I recommend this is because it's so easy to forget much of what's in the book. The glossy wall-chart has been designed to go on the wall of your kitchen (just above where you juice ideally) so you have the *key* mental and physical juice tips on hand every day. To see things even more clearly, make a point of watching the Juice Master Ultimate Fast Food video or, if you have time, come to one of the juicing workshops to learn how to become a master of juice in just a few hours!

One last thing before you read up on all the amazing facts about fruit and veg that will have you saying things like, "stone the grows", "well I never", and "well cover me in blackberries and eat me—I never knew that!" To the many people who say "juicing is a hassle" or "I can't be bothered" or "what's the point" or "eating healthily is a pain in the butt," I want you to listen up, listen hard and do your best to—

AVOID THE WAR

Imagine there's a war going on, and in this war two out of every three people die; even those who do manage to "live" through it are often very ill or disabled due to the enemy's sustained attack. Now imagine you *have* to go. Every man and woman has been called up and you too are on the list. However, there is a way to get a reprieve, a way to avoid this horrific war; you have to breathe properly and make some freshly extracted beautiful juice every day. What do you do? Not exactly tricky to answer is it? All I know is this, it's much, much easier spending ten to twenty minutes a day making juices than it is to spend god knows how many months or years trying to deal with cancer or heart disease! It's amazing how, even if you feel tired, that thought alone will get you juicing in no time. It took Christopher Reeve many months just to learn how to breathe again—how hard is it to make a juice daily, I mean how hard is it to avoid the war— really? All you've got to do is get juiced and get rid of the majority of the rubbish from your diet.

The hard truth is there is a war going on and the casualties are just about everywhere—just take a look around. The problem is we're bombarded with Hollywood and magazine images of "health," but that's not the reality for the majority of people in the Western world. The reality is in every hospital and doctors' office in the country. The reality is that cancer and heart disease are the nation's biggest killers and the *majority* of all degenerative diseases are preventable. Isn't that mad? Most of the people that are in the hospital are *only* there because of what they've been putting into their mouths. That's right. Not for hereditary reasons, or accidents, but as a direct result of overspending on their life accounts; as a direct result of putting the wrong "foods" and "drinks" into their bodies. I'm not picking on them; heaven knows I was there myself for years, and most are in The Food Trap, The Nicotine Trap, or The Alcohol Trap and simply don't know how to get out. Many don't even know they're in it! I just think it's mad that the vast majority of people needing treatment for degenerative disease needn't be there.

According to The World Health Organisation, 85 percent of adult cancers are avoidable!

In the United States, one person dies every thirty three seconds from cardiovascular disease, but research from Cambridge University found that eating just *one apple a day* cuts the risk of premature death from heart disease by 20 percent, add one orange and one banana and it goes up to 50 percent—imagine what two pints of "live" juice would do for you!

John F. Kennedy once famously said, "ask not what your country can do for you—ask what *you* can do for your country." I would like to follow in his wonderful footsteps—

"Ask not what your nation's health services can do for you—ask what *you* can do for your nation's health services"

Hospitals and clinics nationwide are bursting at the seams with millions of casualties and health care costs continue to rise. But remember, health, like most worthwhile things in life, cannot be bought, *you* can only earn it. It's no good spending your life saying "they" haven't found a cure for this or that, "they" won't help us, "they're" not doing enough—one thing you need to realize is that people in the health industry are just normal human beings doing their hardest to try and pick up the pieces after we are *already* ill. It's no good overspending everyday, getting diseased, and then complaining that it's someone else's fault. Personal responsibility is the key to lifelong healthy success.

The truth is you really *can* avoid the war, and by doing so, it frees up some space in the hospitals for people in car crashes, beatings, and *genuine* hereditary factors—the people who really need help, the people who *really* couldn't do anything to help themselves. I have said that juicing is the ultimate insurance policy and every time you have a rich creamy "live" juice you are investing in your very own health service. This in turn helps the health care industry and those who need it most and at the same time helps you to avoid the war.

I truly wish you supreme mental and physical health and a quality of life that many people only dream of.

Keep smiling, design your life, enjoy the journey, drop me a line and
STAY JUICED!

L.I.F.E.

Live an Incredibly Fruity Existence

14

The A–Z Guide to Nature's Fast Foods

 This section features all the fruit, veg, and what I call "vegetable fruits" that you will need for your new fast food way of life. It tells you what to buy, how to store it, how to see if it's ripe, whether it's best for juicing or blending, and exactly how to prepare it. You will notice that not every single fruit and veg is included. This is because not all fruit and veg are suitable for juicing or blending. I have included just the ones I use, the ones in my recipes, and the ones that you will use on a regular basis.

You will also notice that despite what I said in the section entitled "We Don't Need To Know," I have included some nutritional facts. As I've said before, you really *don't* need to know this stuff, but it's there for all of you who like your facts. Also included, by public demand, is some information on what's in your juice and what particular benefits it could give. Again, this is just in case you *want* to know.

Let's Get Fruity

Apple

Contains approximately 85 percent water

An Apple a Day Keeps the Doctor Away

The humble apple is quite simply amazing. OK so it has been linked with the discovery of gravity, but it is also considered to be one of the finest anticancer and health aids ever created. Apples ooze raw life force and contain a "hip-hip-array" of vitamins and minerals—most notably beta-carotene, folic acid, vitamin C, calcium, chlorine, magnesium, phosphorus, potassium, and sulphur. Apples also contain more bioflavinoids than you can shake a tail feather at and are one of the best body cleansers on the planet.

Apples—the Vacuum Cleaner of the Fruit World

Apples contain something called pectin. Once in the body, this incredible stuff forms a gel that helps remove any built-up toxic waste that might be lurking in the very long and windy intestinal tract. Apples are often referred to as the "intestinal broom," but as we are now in the twenty-first century—and given the sheer power they have to lift rubbish clean out of the many nooks and crannies along the thirty feet of intestinal tract—I'd like to rename them "the intestinal vacuum cleaner". Not only do they help to suck out the rubbish, apples also help to flush the kidneys and liver, and keep skin crystal clear. In addition, like all "live" plant food on this planet, they feed every cell in the body and help to build up your defences against disease—pretty incredible considering it's "*just* an apple."

What's best—juice or smoothie?
With apples you can make both. I tend to juice them more—for when it comes to juicing, this little beauty is one of the most versatile there

is. Apple is one of the very few fruits that combine well with just about any fruit or veg and, without them, most vegetable juices would be about as much fun—taste-wise—as an evening with Freddie Kruger! Apples, along with carrots, really are your best friend when it comes to making vegetable juice taste divine—and with numerous varieties available you certainly won't be stuck for choice. Apples also play a huge part in making some of the most wonderful fruit concoctions known to mankind and, if you pardon the pun, will be at the very "core" of your juicing routine. You can even chop them up, put into your blender and mix with just about anything—that way you also get some of the powerful cleansing fiber contained in the whole fruit, but in a liquidized form. (You'll find some examples in the recipe section.)

Apple is one of the fastest of juices to make, especially if you have a juicer that takes whole apples. There is no need to peel, chop or scrub them—even if they are not organic, as most of the "wax" and chemicals used in the growing process are ejected rather cleverly into the pulp jug. If you have a machine with a small chute, it simply means spending slightly more time chopping them to fit the chute in your particular machine.

What are the best apples for juicing?
Personally I love the juice from Royal Gala apples, but having said that, *all* apples juice well. Each one has its own very distinctive flavor, some very sharp, some very sweet, but as there are 1,400 different types, I'm not about to describe each one here. Granny Smiths are a favorite for many, along with Golden Delicious. Try lots of varieties to find your favorite.

The juice is very dark and cloudy—is this normal?
Yep! This is what fresh apple juice should look like. It's the clear stuff you find on the shelves of supermarkets that is completely abnormal. The problem is we've become so used to the clear-looking, pasteurized apple juice that we think totally natural, freshly extracted apple juice is the weird-looking stuff! One thing though, apple juice by itself oxidizes very, very quickly so make certain you drink it IMMEDIATELY after making it. However, if it's mixed with other fruit and veg—

especially if there's lemon or lime somewhere in the equation—it will not oxidize anywhere near as fast. If the juice does start to separate, stir it before drinking.

I've heard the pips contain arsenic. Does this mean I should cut them out before juicing?
No, no, no! Apple pips do contain a minuscule amount of a type of arsenic, but you would have to bathe in them for a month and eat bucket loads of the pips before they presented even a slight problem. Also, there isn't a whole lot of juice in the pips, so you can rest assured that they'll end up in the pulp.

Apricots

Over 85 percent water

Apricots are one of the staple foods of the remote Hunza people of the Himalayas—a people reputed to live to an average age of 120. Not only do most die of natural causes, the majority are still working past their 100th birthday. Of course the Hunza people don't only eat apricots—they also have whole grains, other fruits, and get plenty of fresh air and exercise—but there is no question that the apricot makes an extremely valuable contribution to their health and longevity.

The Beta-Carotene Champions of the Fruit World

Apricots are loaded with the best cancer preventative known to mankind—beta-carotene. In fact, in the fruit world only cantaloupe melon has an equal amount of this amazing substance.

These little orange-gold beauties contain more potassium and magnesium than you can throw a banana at, which help to supply us with energy, stamina, and endurance. The humble apricot is also an excellent blood builder, containing a large amount of iron, and is rich in calcium. And if all that wasn't enough to convince you of the amazing health and vibrancy properties of this Himalayan wonder—it also has stacks of silicon to help your hair shine and your skin glow.

What's best—juice or smoothie?

This will sound a bit strange coming from me—being The Juice Master and all that—but I strongly recommend *not* juicing this fruit. The reason for this is simple—the cost. Apricot juice is really, really nice, but if you want some you may need to talk to your bank manager. Apricots are small, and once you've taken out the seed, you are left with very little fruit—juice it and you'll end up with virtually nothing. You need a hell of a lot of these babies to get a glass of juice, and considering their cost, it just isn't worth it. Plus, when it comes to soft fruits in particular, the "whole" is better than just the juice, as the fiber helps prevent the bloodstream being loaded with too much glucose at once. This tends to be why I eat most of my fruits and drink my veg. When I do have a fruit juice, it tends to nearly always be a smoothie, as these contain "whole" pieces of fruit as well as juice—leaving in plenty of the much-needed daily fiber.

Buying and preparation

When buying apricots look for fruits that are firm, but not hard enough to win a game of conkers with. The outside skin should be orangey-gold and have a very faint but noticeably pinky tinge, which indicates sweetness. They should never be green. Store at room temperature for a few days or in the fridge. If you haven't used them and they are "on the turn," seed and chop them, place in a freezer bag or container, and freeze. Remember, when you freeze fruits you only lose about 5 percent of the live nutrients. The frozen, chopped apricots can then be put into a blender straight from the freezer whenever you want to include them in a smoothie.

Bananas

Surprisingly, over 80 percent water content

Before I explain the natural body-building and energy-giving powers of the humble banana, I want to get something off my chest. The wonderful banana has, over the last twenty to thirty years, received quite a lot of bad press—especially from the slimming clubs—and I would like to help reverse this by explaining very clearly that . . .

Bananas Will Not Make You Fat

Well, perhaps this isn't strictly true—if you ate bucket loads every day and stayed stuck to your sofa 24/7, then yes, me thinks they could and probably would, but then so would just about anything if you did that! Slimming clubs are, to my mind, responsible for many people believing they are better off having a sugar-loaded "light" chocolate bar, than they would be eating a banana. Why do they think this? All because of calories. As I've already mentioned in "We Don't Need to Know," calories don't mean Jack! I could put you on a diet of 4,000 calories a day and you would *lose* weight; I could put you on another diet of 2,000 calories a day and you would *gain* weight—it all depends on the source of the calorie, the usable value, and whether it gets converted into fat once in the body. Alas, many of the slimming organizations aren't that clued up, and with bananas it's quite easy to give them a bad press—why? Because there is no escaping one fundamental fact about these odd-shaped life-savers—they are full of sugar. In fact 22 percent of a banana is sugar, but, and I want to make this very clear—

they're full of the right kind of sugar

Bananas, like a lot of food, will not make you fat if you use them correctly. Bananas are an incredible source of energy, but if you work in an office all day long and don't exercise then you don't want to have a smoothie every day with three bananas in it—that would then have the potential to be converted into fat for future energy use. If you don't then use that energy, then yes it stays as fat—so use your common sense when it comes to this fruit and use it as an energy tool. Eating loads of bananas and banana-type smoothies is for people who need a lot of fuel—runners, body builders, manual workers, and so on. For those running a marathon, forget stuffing yourself with pasta for energy, have a few "power" smoothies instead (see The Hulk Hogain page 226).

The Real Carbo*hydrate*

I never really understood why pasta, bread, rice, etc. came to be called carbo*hydrate*s. The carbo bit yes, but they don't hydrate the body, they rob it of its water supply. Bananas—and all other fruits for that matter—are genuine carbohydrates because they not only supply the body with an excellent source of sugar for immediate and future energy use, but also contain loads of water to help transport the nutrients through the body. And my, what an array of life-giving nutrients we have! These half-moon-shaped instant energy boosters contain bags of amino acids, which are the building blocks of protein. They are also rich in beta-carotene, vitamin B3, folic acid, and vitamin C, and their high mineral content is impressive. Bananas are a particularly good source of potassium, and if you drink tons of water for whatever reason it is advised to eat a banana, as drinking too much water flushes out much-needed potassium from the body.

What's best—juice or smoothie?
BANANAS DO NOT JUICE—BANANAS DO NOT JUICE—BANANAS DO NOT JUICE
As you may have gathered, bananas are not for your juicer. All that comes out is about half an inch of thick gunge—the rest is totally wasted. Either eat bananas, make them into a smooothie or, if you have a Green Life or Champion juicer, you can make instant fruit ice creams by simply putting them through the machine on the homogenizing setting. I have

no idea how it works, but out comes a delicious fruit ice cream. Actually you can make something similar without these machines. Simply take some frozen banana, strawberry, or whatever frozen soft fruit you choose and put, into a blender with some ice—what you will end up with is like a very thick shake that you can eat with a spoon (see Keeping It Cool! recipes page 230). Bananas are also great for making natural milk (see Almond and Banana Milk recipe page 245).

Buying and preparation

When you are buying bananas to use within a few days of purchase, make sure they're ripe. *Never* eat underripe bananas—they are very hard for the body to digest, as the sugars haven't formed naturally yet. Make sure that there are some tiny black dots—these indicate ripeness. Most bananas are actually picked green and then "gassed" to ripeness. Therefore if you have the forethought and time, it's best to buy them green and let them ripen naturally at room temperature. Better still, put them in a paper bag with an apple and put them in a cupboard. The chemical reactions of the two fruits create a natural gas that ripens the bananas in a natural way, very close to if they had been left on a tree, leaving virtually their full mineral content intact. Do not store them in the fridge, but by all means peel, place in a plastic container, and freeze to use in ice creams and smoothies.

Blueberry

Over 80 percent water

Fats Domino once put the words thrill and blueberry in the same sentence and once you taste these tiny blue life-givers, you'll see he was right to do so. Blueberries are one of my favorite fruits to use in a smoothie, especially frozen. Once again nature has provided us with a beautifully colored, sweet tasting, extremely versatile, nutrient-packed fruit that acts as both food and protector. They are rich in vitamin B1, B2, B6, C, biotin, and folic acid.

Every time you consume one of these tiny blue delights you not only feed your cells life-giving nutrients, but you help to build your natural pharmacy. Blueberries are known to fight harmful bacteria and help prevent cancer, as well as helping the body to work synergistically and maintain a natural balance.

What's best—juice or smoothie?

As they are a very small soft fruit and relatively pricey, I recommend that you put them in a blender with other fruits and juices to make a smoothie (see The "No" Fats Domino page 188). Fresh blueberries are available from early summer until late summer/early autumn, and are at their peak in July. The frozen fruits can be used all year round in smoothies and also make delicious ice cream shakes (see Keeping It Cool! recipes for examples). Fresh blueberries are also divine just eaten as they are.

Cherries

Over 80 percent nutrient-rich water

Cherries have been called the "seeds of the future" and one thing is for sure, replace junkie type foods for these little, shiny, very dark red, nutrient-packed beauty fruits and I for one predict a very bright future for you.

These dark red, nutrient-packed little beauties are loaded with the best-known cancer preventative on the planet—yep, 'tis our old friend beta-carotene and all his little carotinoids. Perhaps this is something to do with why *all* wild, fruit-eating primates never seem to get cancer, or come to think of it, any other degenerative diseases that have become so "normal" for us.

Cherries are also packed with folic acid, vitamins C, E, and more Bs than you can shake a hornet at. They also help to replenish your mineral bank accounts with calcium, magnesium, phosphorus, potassium, sulphur, and even small amounts of silicon, copper, iron, and zinc. So there's no chance of a mineral deficiency if you eat plenty of these babies. (All these benefits also apply to plums, peaches, and apricots—which are members of the same family). They also help to prevent build up of plaque—so they're excellent for your teeth too!

What's best—juice or smoothie?

Like most fruits, you can of course do both, but as they are a small fruit, I tend to either eat them or take out the middle seed and blend them into a smoothie or ice cool shake. Having said that, cherry juice is beautiful and is definitely worth the expense once in a while.

Buying and preparation

Cherries do not continue to ripen after they are removed from their umbilical cord, the tree—so look for firm, shiny cherries and skip the ones that are either rock-hard or mushy. You also want to look for darker fruits, as their mineral content is higher.

To prepare, simply take out the seed and put into juicer or blender for the drink of your choice. Once again if you have loads you can seed and freeze them for later use. They're perfect for use in The Hanni"ball" (page 231)—just replace the black grapes with frozen cherries.

Cranberry

Nearly 90 percent nutrient-packed, life-giving water

The cranberry is another fruit that has received its fair share of bad press; this time not because it's accused of making you fat, but because of its high acid content. While researching these berries, I was surprised to meet with conflicting views from two of my mentors—Jay Kordich and Dr. Norman Walker, one of the true pioneers of juicing. According to Jay, "Drinking fresh cranberry juice is one of the best things you can do," while the late, great Dr. Walker once stated, "Unless you have a liver or kidney disturbance, they should be avoided completely." So where do I stand? Well, with both of them! How so?

Probably over 85 percent of all people in the Western World have been consuming what I describe as a "junkie diet" for many years. Over 80 percent drink alcohol on a very regular basis and over 96 percent drink either tea or coffee every single day. Add to this the highly processed, fat-, salt-, and sugar-laden foods that the majority of people consume every week and you are almost guaranteed a battered and bruised liver and kidneys. Cranberry juice contains something called quinine, otherwise known as quininic acid. This stuff is so powerful that, once in the liver, it converts to another acid that helps to lift toxins not only from the bladder and kidneys but also the prostate and testicles. So if you are already in great health, there really is no need to have cranberry juice, as it will probably do more harm than good. However, if you *already* have liver, kidney, prostate, or bladder problems—which is very likely given the usual Western diet—it's a great little fruit to have in your natural pharmacy department. The positive effect cranberry has on liver and kidney function also makes it an excellent juice for people with skin disorders.

You Little Tart!

Cranberries are, to put it mildly, a little tart (it's the quinine acid that makes them taste bitter)—so I personally never drink the juice by itself. When using cranberries in a juice, always mix them with a sweeter-tasting juice—apple is best. In fact what's known as "cranapple" juice is really nice.

What's best—juice or smoothie?
It's totally up to you on this one. Personally I do both, depending on what I feel like and the purpose of the drink. If I'm treating a liver/kidney disturbance then I'll make a "cranapple" juice, but if I just want a tasty drink, I'll just add a few frozen cranberries to a smoothie.

Buying and preparation
The cranberry season kicks off around November and lasts over the festive season. Buy them fresh and then freeze them so you can have

access to these extremely beneficial fruits all winter long. There's no need to prepare these fruits at all—just wash them before making your juice or smoothie.

Grapefruit

Over 80 percent water

 The Grapefruit—a fruit that looks nothing like a grape and isn't even from the same family. Still, these round pink, red, and white beauties make a great juice and combine well with all other fruits to make some beautiful smoothies.

Life Really Is the Piths!

Once again we find that not only do these amazing fruits taste good, but hiding just beneath their tough outer protective skin, is one of the most potent and beneficial substances in nature's pharmacy—the pith! Yep, that white, sometimes stringy stuff found on the inside of the skin and outside of the fruit is packed with life force—an absolute cavalcade of vitamins and minerals—and that's before you get into what's in the fruit. One of the many all-round unbelievable feats they can perform on the inner sanctuary of your wellness is the ability to help break down and shift INORGANIC calcium that may have formed deposits in the cartilage of the joints—apparently it's the "salicylic acid" that does this.

Holy Cow! I Didn't Know That

One of the many attributes of the grapefruit is its ability to help break down and shift inorganic calcium deposits in the cartilage of the joints. Despite what we have been taught over the years, dairy products, of all things, can play a part in the buildup of this inorganic calcium—could have something to do with the fact that cow's milk was designed for calves not humans! The good news is the calcium found in fruits like grapefruits is fully utilized by the body and doesn't cause such problems. Grapefruits also contain bucket loads (well not quite!) of Vit C and are another excellent source of our cancer-fighting agent—beta-carotene. If all that wasn't enough, they also have high levels of pectin, which is known to control cholesterol levels and help digestive problems.

But I've heard they are very acidic, is that true?
Yep—but the acids in this fruit are good. They help to stimulate digestion as well as zap deposits in the joints. What may come as somewhat of a surprise is that grapefruit—just like all acid-tasting fruits (with the exception of cranberries)—has an *alkalizing* effect once it is in the body.

I find the taste a bit sour, so should I skip them?
Like everything, there are so many different fruits and veg that all feed the body, cleanse, and help to protect it that if you really don't like something you can just skip it. Do give them a try first, though. I personally hate grapefruits on their own, but love them mixed with other fruits in a juice or smoothie. However, do not do what so many people do and add white refined sugar to try and "improve" the taste.

What's best—juice or smoothie?
Juice, juice, juice. By all means you can add the juice to your blender and mix with soft whole fruits, but I wouldn't advise putting the whole fruit in a smoothie.

Buying and preparation
When buying, you are looking for a "springy" feel, not mushy and soft, and it should be flat at both ends. Before juicing, simply peel them, remembering to leave the outer white pith on. If you are in a hurry and have a citrus juicer, simply cut the fruit in half and place on the rotator—however, bear in mind that you will not get the benefits of the pith if you do this.

Grapes

Over 85 percent life-supplying water

 Where do we start with these little gems? Do we talk about their ability to help calm the nervous system as few other fruits do? Or do we mention the incredible mineral content that helps to strengthen the alkaline reserves in the body, promotes good bowel movement and proper kidney function, and regulates the heartbeat? What about the terrific amount of iron that builds hemoglobin in the blood? Or the fact that they're rich in vitamins C and E? It really is hard to know where to start with these extremely beneficial juicy fruits.

The Food of the Gods

Grapes have long been described as the food of the gods, and there is no doubt that these amazing fruits are a blessing. It seems man has praised them for a long time too—grape seeds were even found in Egyptian tombs! Today they appear to have not lost any of their following. In France, many people go through spats of eating nothing but grapes (known as mono-dieting) during the grape season in order to cleanse the system and rebalance the body's acid/alkaline levels. And in Germany there are "fasting clinics" where people are put on a diet of nothing but grapes for seven days. As you may have guessed, they have superb results for all kinds of ailments, especially for those with arthritis. Grapes are one of the best cleansers on the market and also help to stimulate the metabolism.

What's best—juice or smoothie?
Juice, juice, juice.

Buying and preparation
When buying grapes there are a few things you need to look out for.

Firstly do your best to get either organic or something called "spray-free" grapes. I am very fortunate as where I live in East Dulwich, London, there is a little ole fashioned greengrocers where they sell tons of genuine organic produce from their own farm. Some commercial growers will use up to forty different pesticides and chemicals—so be careful! That doesn't mean don't have them if you cannot get organic—they will still be very good for you, especially once juiced, as a lot of the skin goes in the pulp anyway.

When it comes to appearance, look for firm, well-colored fruits. When you pick up a bunch none should drop off, they shouldn't be leaking or mushy or have dried-up brown stems—all this indicates that the grapes are too old.

Grapes don't require any preparation—simply put everything, including the stem, through your machine. If the juice tastes too sweet, which can be the case, add lemon, lime, or apple juice, perhaps even all three.

JM TIP: Do not drink grape juice while eating any cooked food. If you want to get maximum benefit from these fruits, wait fifteen to thirty minutes and then eat if necessary.

NOTE: IF YOU ARE DIABETIC OR SUFFER FROM HYPOGLYCEMIA DO NOT DRINK GRAPE JUICE

Grape juice is very high in natural sugars, which will be rapidly absorbed into the bloodstream. Those with blood sugar problems should therefore avoid it, but even those without such problems should ensure they add a little water to the juice and sip it slowly. This applies to all fruit juices but is particularly important with grape juice. Remember that digestion starts in the mouth, so "swill" and "chew" your juice.

Kiwi Fruit

Over 70 percent nutrient-packed water

Fortunately, largely thanks to the Wright brothers! there is no need to go "down under" to get hold of these little green and gold beauties—but given just how scrumptious and beneficial they are to health, it would have certainly been worth the trip! Yep, as you may have guessed from the name, the kiwi fruit does indeed come from New Zealand. It actually originated and was created from a much less tastier fruit called—the Chinese gooseberry. The farmers of NZ were very proud of their creation and named it after the country's national bird—the Kiwi, which, unlike the Wrights, never learned to fly!

Once again nature has provided a food, a protector, and a natural medicine all in one little package. Whether gold or green they are packed with beta-carotene and even contain twice as much vitamin C as oranges. On the mineral front, they are rich in calcium, magnesium, phosphorus, potassium, and sodium.

When it comes to juicing and smoothies they are simply a must. Kiwi juice is one of the tastiest juices of all—it has been described as a mixture of pineapple and strawberries—and, because you don't need to peel the fruit, it's also one of the fastest to make. No chopping, no peeling, just pop in the chute and boom—beautiful kiwi juice in seconds.

What's best—juice or smoothie?

This truly versatile fruit makes fantastic juice and is a great addition to smoothies. Obviously, depending on time of year, kiwi juice could work out a tad expensive. If so, use them to make smoothies.

Buying and preparation

Look for firm fruits, but ones that also give slightly when squeezed. When making kiwi juice you don't have to peel them, even if they're not organic—just juice and go! If, however, you're putting them in a blender, you should take the outer skin off, as it may contain chemicals and can be a little harsh on the back of the throat. You can also peel and freeze—frozen kiwi, mixed with frozen strawberry, banana, and a little lime juice and ice makes one hell of a thick ice shake.

Lemons and Limes

Over 90 percent alkalizing water

Lemons and limes are from the same family—very close cousins apparently—and both play an important role in juicing. With a taste sharper than Chris Rock's tongue, these little citrus toxin blasters help to add zest and bite to any fruit or vegetable concoction.

The Fruit Olympics

If there were a fruit Olympics and the event was "maintaining the body's natural balance" there is no question that lemons and limes would be wearing gold. They would also be in the final for "cleansing the body" and "eliminating toxins" and would win gold in the "neutralizing bad bacteria" competition. In fact, one Charles Richet is said to have discovered that lemon juice added to raw oysters destroys 92 percent of the bacteria present within just fifteen minutes. So as you can see they do much more than just prevent scurvy.

Lemon juice in particular, especially when mixed with warm water, is one of the best therapies there is for use in all cases of infection of the respiratory tract and as a general tonic. It has an incredible alkalizing effect on the body and helps to calm the central nervous system. Lemons and limes contain four times the amount of citric acid of oranges and grapefruits—this amazing acid is wonderful for pushing out toxins from the body, usually through the skin, which makes them valuable in treating fevers.

Lemons and limes mix with any fruit juice and, in small amounts, any vegetable juice. Adding a good squeeze of lemon or lime to your juice can also help to slow down the rate at which it oxidizes—this is very similar to adding lemon juice to an already open avocado to stop it going brown.

I cannot say enough about these fruits, even the skin is excellent for bites and stings! If you want better health I would certainly include these beauties somewhere into your daily diet. They are cheap, and because they are so potent, go a long way. I believe, considering how versatile they are and what they do, they are the best value fruit around.

What's best—juice or smoothie?

Juicing is best (though my favorite is simply cutting them into chunks and putting them in water). You can, if you wish, also peel them and add small chunks to a smoothie or ice cool shake to add a bit of zest.

Buying and preparation

When buying lemons, look for fruit that are plump and heavy for their size and have no hint of green (this indicates they are under-ripe). When buying limes, look for those that are the lightest green.

Unlike their citrus friends orange, grapefruit, and tangerine, the skins of both lemons and limes are digestible. This means there is no need to peel them before juicing. However, having said that, if you juice with skin on, the juice can be a little sharp. Try with and without to see which you prefer. If you are going to juice with the skin on it's worth investing in a biodegradable produce wash and small scrubbing brush to help get off the wax and chemicals. If buying organic there is no need to do this. The best place to keep them is in a cool place, though not as cold as your fridge.

Mango

Over 75 percent totally tropical live water

 Mmmmmm, gorgeous, lovely, scrumptious, delicious, delightful, tantalizing—a true taste bud's dream. There are few fruits in the world that taste and smell as good as a ripe mango, and they are so effective as an internal body cleaner that they'll even have you smelling sweeter. Yep, these babies are known to be "the body disinfectants" of the fruit world and can actually be extremely effective against body odor.

May the Force Be with You

Much more importantly, mangoes are not short in the vitamin and mineral departments. They're rich in beta-carotene, vitamin C, and contain many B vitamins; and are a good source of calcium, magnesium, and potassium. They are also packed with antioxidants, or "free radical police" as I call them, helping to find, calm, and stabilize any molecule that's gone haywire in cellular city. In short, without antioxidants preventing the mass slaughter of our trillions of cells, we would perish. Of course, if your diet largely consists of junk foods and drinks, then the body ends up having a free radical riot. The good news is that all fruit and veg are loaded with tons of "riot police" and mangoes are just one of the tastiest ways to get this "force" working for you.

What's best—juice or smoothie?

For many, the juice from a mango is too thick and can work out pretty pricey, as you don't get a great deal of juice from it (this varies according to which machine you are using). It does, however, make excellent "mixer" juice. I personally recommend putting mango in your blender and making some of the finest smoothies on the planet—for an example, try the Caribbean Dream on page 181.

If you do happen to own a Champion or Green Life juicer, try putting some frozen mango through the chute on the homogenizer mode, add some frozen pineapple and banana and you will have created one of the most delicious and healthiest desserts in the world.

If you do juice a mango, to create one the richest and creamiest juices there is, make sure you mix it with another juice (like pineapple) or blend it with plenty of ice.

Buying and preparation

Look for fruits that are yellowish green with a red blush to them. When buying mangoes, look for the larger ones, as they tend to be juicier. They should give slightly when squeezed and should smell divine at the stem end. Reject any mango that is rock hard or mushy. Mangoes should be stored at room temperature so that they continue to ripen. Once cut, however, the best place for them is in the fridge.

The only drawback the mango has is the whopping great flat stone running through the middle of it. This isn't a problem when you "eat off the stone" as I say, but for chopping purposes it can be a bit of pain until you get the hang of it. The trick is to put the mango on its side, get a very sharp knife and place it dead centre. Then just shift the knife a little to the right or left and cut down. If you cannot cut down you are hitting the stone, so just move over a tiny fraction, then do the same on the other side. You can then scoop out the flesh from the skin with a spoon. If the fruit is a little hard, you can peel it with a knife as you would a potato. Hard to explain, but if you ever get the chance to see my video, you'll get the full picture.

Melons

Anything up to 95 percent mineral-rich, life-giving, body-cooling water

As Cool as a Cucumber and from the Same Family Too

The cleansing and cooling effect of melon is unsurpassed in the fruit world—they are quite simply amazing. You could take the top scientists from all over the world and put them in a lab for twenty years and still they wouldn't be able to come up with anything that could flush, clean, feed, and protect the body like a melon—not because they are stupid, it's just that nature is so ingenious!

There are many, many different types of melon to be found across the globe, but two melons, cantaloupe and watermelon came out on top in a "most nutritious fruit" list compiled by the Center for Science in the Public Interest. Personally I'm loath to put fruit in any order of merit, as each has its own unique properties as well as plenty we may not yet have discovered, so a list of this kind seems somewhat, well . . . fruitless! But it does mean that of all the nutrients we *can* identify, melons come out on top.

My "Rind" of Fruit

What may come as a bit of a surprise is that most of the identified nutrients are in fact to be found in the rind of the melon. In fact, a reported whopping 95 percent of all the nutrients in any melon are to be found in some part of the rind and this is why juicing them is soooo fantastic. Juicing extracts the very valuable vitamins and minerals that would otherwise benefit the soil and not us. And when it comes to minerals, melons are right up there with the best of them. Their tremendous root systems reach so deep into the soil that they are able to withdraw massively from nature's mineral bank acount, which, once eaten, helps to add to our body's life account very nicely.

Skin Deep

These mineral-rich fruits are, like many of their cousins, superb kidney cleaners and skin purifiers. Watermelons, for example, not only have the highest water content of all fruits, they also contain plenty of the mineral world's dynamic duo—zinc and potassium. Once again, these are to be found very close to the rind, so when you juice these babies you reap *all* the benefits—clearer skin, harder nails, shiny healthy hair, and more energy than you can shake a pip at. If you want to purify your skin so it glows, forget using expensive creams on the outside and let the toxin-blasting powers of this incredible fruit make your skin glow from the inside.

JM TIP: If you have a skin condition such as psoriasis or eczema, it usually means on top of a clogged system, you more than likely have a very large mineral deficiency. Although these fruits are loaded with much needed zinc, I would strongly recommend a further supplement of 100 mgs of zinc (twice daily) and 400 mgs of selenium (twice daily). As you already know, I'm not a big fan of supplements, as most are completely unnecessary, but in this case they can be of huge benefit. Just so you know the best natural source of these two minerals—it's brazil nuts, so get munching!

What's best—juice or smoothie?

I personally don't think you can beat simply eating cool slices of melon on a hot day. However, as 95 percent of the vitamin and mineral content is to found very close to and in the rind itself, these beauties should be juiced at every opportunity. If you want to add cool chunks of frozen melon to a smoothie then feel free, just make certain you don't freeze the chunks of melon with the rind. All in all, the best bet is to eat cool slices and have a glass of the rind juice with it.

Buying and preparation

When buying a watermelon, knock it with your knuckles and if it sounds hollow, it's ripe and ready to eat. Make sure the skin is dull—it shouldn't be shiny. You should also be able to scratch off the green skin with your fingernails easily—another sign that it is ripe, sweet, and ready to eat (or juice). With all other types of melon, you should look for fruit that sounds hollow and smells sweet. When it comes to preparing them for juicing, nothing could be easier—simply cut them into pieces and put the lot through your juicer.

JM TIP: Melons and melon juice are so high in water that they flush through the system very, very quickly. Because of this I *strongly* advise that you have it by itself, without interference from any other food. The ideal time is when your stomach is empty, but if you feel like some when out for dinner, have some *before* your main dish. Never have it after dinner. If you do this it will sit with the other food and begin to ferment, which is not good.

Nectarines

Over 85 percent peachy, water-rich liquid

Chinese Delight

 We have China to thank for these little balls of delight, for 'tis where they originate. This gorgeous fruit is very aptly named, for when it comes to taste they are most definitely pure nectar. The nectarine is, as you may have guessed, related to the peach. However, unlike the peach, it has a smooth rather than velvety skin and, with its bright red and orange appearance, is more colorful. And when it comes to making beautiful smoothies and juices, the nectarine is a little more versatile and cost effective than the peach—in fact the only thing the peach has over its cousin is the taste and even then it's fairly close. The liquid nectar from this fruit, when drank by itself or mixed with others in a juice or smoothie is not only totally taste-bud-tastic, but feeds the cells, mops up free-radicals, flushes the system, and helps oxygen flow to the cells.

Free or Cling?

Like many fruits that have a stone in the centre, the nectarine comes in either something called freestone or clingstone. This is somewhat self-explanatory—clingstone means the fruit literally clings to the fruit and freestone means the fruit falls away freely from the stone. The most common variety is the freestone.

And For Those Who Want To Know

Here are the stats on nectarines . . . They're rich in beta-carotene; they make a good showing on the vitamin front with folic acid, vitamin C, and small amounts of B1, B2, B3, B5, and B6; and on the mineral side of things they boast calcium, magnesium, phosphorus, potassium, and traces of copper, iron, magnesium, and zinc.

What's best—juice or smoothie?

Nectarines can be a very good value, especially compared to their much-loved cousin the peach. Because it is a pretty firm fruit, it juices very well, though you do of course need a few to make a decent glass, but it is well worth it for it tastes delicious. It can be a bit thick by itself, so I recommend mixing it with other juices, especially pineapple. Nectarine is also good in smoothies—just cut into chunks, pop in your blender with some juice, some other fruits, and a bit of ice and you have a smoothie that's pure nectar.

Buying and preparation

When buying nectarines, as with most fruits, do a smell test. Fruits should always have a fruity smell about them. When it comes to the feel test, you want firm but not hard. Wrinkles, cracked skin, and spots are all evidence of decay, so skip these and go for fruits that are blemish free and have a bright, deep coloring. If you can only buy hard fruits, keep them at room temperature and they will soon ripen. If you don't have the patience, then put them in a paper bag with an unripe banana—the gases it produces helps speed up the ripening process.

Preparation is easy; simply cut in half, remove the stone, and juice or blend—no need to peel. If juicing, remember to put the fruit through the chute slowly in order to extract more juice.

Oranges

Over 87 percent mineral-rich, vitamin-packed water

As you embark on your juicing journey you will get to know this extremely versatile fruit very well indeed. In fact, along with carrots and apples, these sweet-tasting babies will become one of your top buys. If you have a family and manage to convert them (which won't be too difficult given how beautiful the juice tastes) you may well find yourself getting in a case of these very juicy fruits on a weekly basis.

Oranges yield plenty of juice, so pure orange juice is one of the most cost-effective juices you can make. If you are serious about your health and investing in your juice kitchen, you can get yourself a separate citrus juicer. This is great if you are in a hurry, as you simply cut the oranges in half, put them on the spinning thing (whatever it's called!), and bingo—juice in seconds with very, very little washing up. If you wish, you can then add the juice to your blender to make a delicious smoothie—all in no time at all.

Juice Pithout the Real Goodness

Like a number of other fruits, the real nutritional magic of the orange is to be found just under the rind—in the pith, the white stringy stuff beneath the peel. For this reason it's best to peel them carefully, leaving on as much pith as possible—it tastes so much better too. Of all juices, freshly extracted orange juice is something you have more than likely tried, although the chances are it came from a commercial citrus juicing machine. Just wait till you've tried the rich, very creamy juice you get from juicing the fruit and the pith—you'll be converted for life. Doing it this way may take a little longer, but good things really do come to those who wait—and my, what good things lie behind that outer layer. Oranges may well have found fame for their vitamin C content, but there are many things you may not know about this humble fruit.

Oranges contain antioxidants that help destroy the free radicals that age the skin and cause premature wrinkles and sagging. Their high citric acid content helps to clean the clogged rubbish from your digestive system and flush the toxins and acid wastes in the cells. In addition, these heaven-sent life enhancers are loaded with that anticancer beta-carotene stuff and, in case you want to know, are a good source of calcium—yes calcium in an orange! They also have plenty of wonderful minerals, including potassium and phosphorus. But it's the vitamin C that made them famous, and for good reason; they are packed with the stuff. It's a good thing too, as the body cannot store this vitamin. Here's something else worth knowing—vitamin C helps iron to be absorbed more easily in the body, and a glass of freshly extracted orange juice a day can double the amount of iron available for use in the body.

What's best—juice or smoothie?

Most definitely juice. You can cut them into chunks and put in your blender, but I wouldn't recommend it—they're a bit too stringy. You can, however, use orange juice as an excellent base for many smoothies—simply put loads of soft fruits in your blender, pour on some orange juice as a base, add some ice, and boom, you have magic in a glass.

Buying and preparation

"Small ones are more juicy" as the saying goes and perhaps for good reason. The only problem is that if you buy small ones you have more to peel. I personally go for large or medium oranges—they still give you plenty of juice. As a rough guide five to six oranges will give you about a pint of creamy juice. To prepare for juicing, simply peel the oranges with a sharp knife, leaving on as much of the pith as possible, then put through the juicer.

NOTE: The orange juice you find in shops has always been pasteurized and therefore is far inferior to that you make yourself.

Papaya

Over 87 percent tropical water

Ladies and Gentlemen, please take a bow: the papaya, or pawpaw, is quite simply the digestive king of the fruit world. These tropical, hand grenade-shaped, pink, fleshy fruits are an amazingly rich source of proteolytic enzymes (nice name!). These are the chemicals that enable the easy digestion of complex proteins such as meat. One of the most important and well known of these enzymes is papain, which is so effective that it is often used as a meat tenderizer. So if you fancy some chicken, have some chunks of papaya with it and give your body a break from having to withdraw from its own enzyme account. In the tropics, this fruit, along with mango and pineapple, is often served with meat and fish dishes.

As with all fruits, the papaya contains an amazing array of vitamins (most notably beta-carotene and vitamin C) and minerals. And its uses don't end there—the skin is a first class external treatment for skin wounds.

It Keeps You Going

Many people have hailed papaya as a great rejuvenator, as it is said to combat premature aging. This is more than likely due to the fact that poor digestion leads to malnourished cells, while efficient digestion ensures that cells are properly fed. Papayas also contain enzymes that are known to be essential for male fertility and others that are good for the heart and circulation—so make mine a pint!

What's best—juice or smoothie?
As they are a soft fruit, quite small, and relatively expensive, it doesn't make economic sense to juice them. On top of that the juice you get, like that of mango, is very thick and would always need thinning with another juice such as orange or pineapple—so I recommend cutting into chunks and throwing into a blender for a smoothie. When mixed whole, this fruit is an excellent source of fiber.

Buying and preparation
When buying papayas look for some yellowing in among the usual green—this indicates that it's on its way to being ripe. To check if it's fully ripe, squeeze it like you would an avocado or mango—if it gives a little, it's ready. As this fruit is at home in the tropics, the fridge is not its best friend, so only keep it cool for a few days.

To prepare papaya, simply cut the fruit in half, scoop out the tiny black seeds, and throw them away (this is optional, you can juice it with them but I find it too bitter). Now spoon out the soft pink flesh, cut into chunks, and chuck into blender, then add some juice from another fruit and whatever else takes your fancy. If the fruit isn't fully ripe, cut the skin off with a knife instead of cutting in half, then just take out the seeds and cut the flesh into chunks.

Peaches

Contains 88 percent pure liquid heaven

Alexander the Truly Great

Like its cousin the nectarine, the peach originated in China, but we have the Greeks and a bloke called Alexander, who was apparently great, to thank for bringing them to our neck of the woods. And I for one am as pleased as punch they did. Of all the mono-juices I have ever made, peach is without question my favorite. I doubt if you will ever get round to making every recipe in the back of this book, chances are once you get used to juicing you'll be conjuring up your very own masterpieces, but I urge you to make a point of at least making A Real Peach on page 192— you'll be very glad you did. It's a mixture of pure peach juice plus whole peaches blended together with a little ice—pure liquid heaven!

A Peach of a Fighter . . . or Should That Be Phyto?

Nature has once again—in the form of an innocent-looking peach— loaded an incredibly mouth-watering fruit with a whole host of those phyto (meaning plant) nutrients. These little babies act as both nurturer and protector. They literally have the ability to fight and prevent disease, and that includes cancer—yes cancer! This why I call them "Fight-o-nutrients." The wonderful news is *all* fruits and veg contain heaps of these little fighters—including, of course, the juicy peach.

Not Just a Pretty Taste!

Yep, the peach might have had plenty of excellent press on the taste front, but when people tend to talk health it's the ole apple, orange, and carrot that seem to grab the headlines. OK so the peach might be greatly appreciated on the taste front, but it is also simply packed with vitamins and minerals galore. The headline-grabbing phytonutrient has simply got to be our old friend beta-carotene, followed rapidly by folic acid and vitamin C and vitamin B3, with even many of the B vitamins making a guest appearance, and that's all without the most powerful one of all—vitamin and mineral X. Yep 'tis that X factor again that makes all fruits and veggies simply X-traordinary, X-ceptional and so X-citing. With that in mind, don't concern yourself with exactly what vits and mins are in this fruit, just be assured that the X factor will, as always, be very present. In fact Chinese legend says that peaches bestow immortality, but I believe all who started that rumour are now dead, so I wouldn't read too much into that one!

Peach Highlights

Very alkalizing and cleansing to the intestinal tract
Encourages good bowel movement
Has both a laxative and a diuretic quality
Helps cleanse the bladder and kidneys
Drinking peach juice can improve your skin and eyesight
Peach juice can help prevent morning sickness

What's best—juice or smoothie?
Pure peach juice can work out to be very expensive, so, unless you wake up sneezing fifty-dollars bills out your nose, I strongly suggest

putting the whole delicious soft fruit into a blender (minus the stone, of course) and making some kind of peach smoothie (see recipes at the back). If you can afford it and feel like a treat once in a while, then have a glass of pure peach juice with some ice—it's gorgeous.

Buying and preparation

When buying peaches, look for fruits that are neither too soft nor too hard. You want fairly firm fruits, but ones that give slightly. Don't press them like you would an avocado as your fingers will go into the fruit and you'll be kicked out of the shop! Also look out for dark bruises, as these can penetrate the fruit to some depth and so ruin most the fruit—given their price it's worth looking for the best. To prepare for juicing or blending simply cut in half, take out the seed, and either put through your juicer or add to the blender.

Pears

Over 85 percent vitamin-rich, body-cleansing water

You Can't Beat a Good Juicy Pear

I once heard the very funny British comedian Eddy Izzard mention the pear in one of his sketches. There is no way that the written word can even begin to capture the brilliance of the sketch, but he observed how when you buy pears they are often rock hard, you then put them in your fruit bowl waiting for them to soften . . . and you wait and you wait and you wait until . . . mush! It must have driven that partridge mad (you know the one in the tree). I must say, I totally empathize with Eddy and that is why I love to juice these often annoying fruits. There is no question that, if you can find one, a ripe juicy pear is one of the tastiest fruits you will ever have the pleasure of dribbling down your chin—it's just finding one that's the problem.

Simple Pear Necessities of Life

Most people I meet have never tasted pear juice, and if you are one of them you are in for a real treat. Pear juice goes a long way too—even the ones that are rock hard will produce loads of thick, sweet, and creamy juice. In fact, if anything, it's a tad too thick and can even be too sweet—this is why I suggest mixing pear juice with other fruits, such as orange and perhaps whole banana (again see recipes). Like apple, pear juice begins to deteriorate very, very quickly, so make sure you drink it as soon as you make it.

Pear Essentials

Pears are a valuable source of vitamins and minerals—most notably vitamins B6 and C, and copper. These babies are great news for diabetics too, as their sweet flavor is largely the result of levulose, a fruit sugar more easily tolerated by people with the condition than others.

Variety—the Spice of Life

Pears have been cultivated for over 3,000 years and there is no shortage of choice. Here are the top three for delicious juices:

Conference When it comes to pear juice you'll see in the recipes I choose this variety over the rest, but you can substitute if they're unavailable in your area. It is rich, sweet, creamy, and mixes well with other fruit juices. It won an award at the 1885 international pear conference and hence became the "conference" pear.
Comice Many believe this to be the best-tasting pear there is and, when it comes to eating them, I have to agree. In fact these pears get their name from the phrase *doyenne du comice*, meaning "top of the show". However, for juicing, they come in a close second to the conference. These pears originate in France and have a yellow-green or russeted

skin, ripening to pinkish-brown. The flesh is smooth, juicy, and a warm, creamy white.

Bartlett This pear is also known as the Williams pear. Available from summer to autumn, their bright yellow skin and sweet taste are extremely inviting. Once again, they are great to eat when fully ripe—juiced they are also divine.

What's best—juice or smoothie?

They are best juiced, although you can include them in a smoothie with other fruits.

Buying and preparation

If you are buying pears to juice rather than eat, you need firm fruits (not too difficult as trying to get ripe pears is about as tricky as finding a parking spot in Manhattan). To juice, simply break off the stem and put the whole fruit through your machine—simple, easy, and delicious. If you want to include pears in a smoothie, cut into chunks before adding to the blender.

Pineapple

Over 85 percent liquid sunshine

South America, Thailand, India, Malaysia, Hawaii, the Caribbean . . . what do all these places have in common? Yes indeedy, they are all home to one of the finest-tasting fruits in the world—the pineapple. Historically considered a symbol of hospitality, the pineapple is one of the most versatile fruits when it comes to creating juices and smoothies. If the only pineapple juice you have ever tasted is the denatured, pasteurized liquid on your supermarket shelves, you are in for one massive treat. The pure, tropical, creamy liquid you get when you freshly extract the juice from this prickly-looking fruit is in a different league to the carton stuff. On the taste front, only pure peach juice is on a par with the juicy pineapple. Mix the two juices together and the result is simply orgasmic.

One Hell of a Smoothie

Pineapple juice on its own is beautiful, make no mistake, but this fruit will go with just about any combination of fruit juice/smoothie and you can even mix it with vegetable juice (and trust me you'll want to). You can cut the fruit into chunks, freeze them, and add to any fruit juice to make a cool creamy smoothie. Alternatively, you can put just the chunks into a blender to produce an ice–cream–type dessert—the kids just love it. Pineapple juice is also a great base for other smoothies—just put your juice in a blender, add some soft fruits and ice, and bingo you have tropical heaven in a glass.

Not Just a Smooth Operator

Like papaya and some other tropical fruits, pineapple contains protein-digesting enzymes. The main one in pineapple is an enzyme called bromelain—this stuff is so powerful it is capable of digesting 1,000 times its weight of protein. (Perhaps this is why you see so many meat dishes in the tropics served with certain fruits and maybe the reason we have pineapple with cheese.) This enzyme also helps dissolve excess mucus and thus relieves asthma and hay fever. In addition, pineapple helps to restore the body's acid/alkaline levels, soothes sore throats, and has even been found to cure laryngitis. Pineapples are also packed with an array of vitamins, minerals, natural fats, amino acids (building blocks for protein), water, and natural sugars.

What's best—juice or smoothie?
Although it can work out pricey, I highly recommend freshly extracted pineapple juice—it really is divine. That doesn't mean you cannot simply put chunks into a blender, add more fruit and make some of the finest smoothies around—you can. I just personally really love the fresh juice.

Buying and preparation

Pineapples do not ripen after they have been harvested—so make sure you get a nice ripe one. Avoid green fruits and have a sniff—they should smell nice and sweet. If the pineapple is cold and hard due to refrigeration, it may not have much of a smell, so simply try to pull one of the green leaves out of the top—if it comes out easily, it's ripe.

You will need a very sharp knife for this fruit. Place the fruit on its side and cut off the top and tail. Then sit it on its base and carefully cut the skin off with a knife, taking off as little of the flesh as possible. Cut the pineapple flesh into pieces small enough to fit in your juicer. If you can find an organic pineapple there is no need to peel—just chop, juice, and go!

Raspberry

Over 85 percent delicious, sweet, life-giving water

 All berries are simply wonderful, each one adding its own unique tantalizing taste and vibrant color to any juice or smoothie. And the tangy, sharp taste and beautiful red color of raspberry is certainly no exception. These tiny balls of delight make an excellent mono-juice, but really come into their own when added to other fruits and juices to make rich smoothies. They are also amazing when frozen and pushed through a Green Life or Champion, along with banana and mango, to make a beautiful ice cream-like dessert.

Raspberries are packed with vitamins and minerals—beta-carotene, vitamin C, calcium, magnesium, phosphorus, and sodium.

What's best—juice or smoothie?

Like all berries, I strongly recommend adding these beautiful fruits to your blender to make smoothies. However, if you find your local greengrocer selling off a load cheap at the end of a day, then raspberry juice is sweet, creamy, and delicious.

When buying, look for the freshest you can get—they should be plump, brightly colored, and not too soft. If you live near a farm and can pick them yourself, wonderful. Raspberries need no preparation other than a quick rinse. Simply mix with other fruits and juices in a blender. Raspberries can also be frozen and are an excellent addition to any smoothie or natural ice cream from a Green Life or Champion juicer.

Strawberries
(The Only Fruit with Its Pips on the Outside—Well I Never!)

Over 90 percent water

A non mover on the berry charts for the past umpteen thousand years, strawberries remain at number one for the 10,000th week running! Yep, of all the berries in the world, strawberries are quite simply the best. The Beatles once sang "Strawberry Fields forever" and I for one second that statement. When I think of strawberries I immediately think of summer. Unfortunately, many people get hold of this lovely summer fruit, add spoonfuls of white refined sugar, then pour loads of artery-clogging cream over them—all to help improve them apparently! I suggest keeping them as nature intended or blending these beauties with some of nature's other marvels (see Glad-it's-Night and the Pips page 223).

Berry Good for You

Like most berries, strawberries are an incredible source of life-giving nutrients. Topping the bill are vitamin C and our old cancer-preventing beauty—beta-carotene. On the mineral front we have bone- and teeth-loving calcium, and potassium and iron. These little mineral babes are magnificent blood builders. Sodium also makes a good showing, helping to calm the nerves and keep our glands healthy. Strawberries are also one of the few fruit juices that contain natural painkillers, some of which form the basis of synthetic drugs like aspirin.

Strawberries also contain something called "ellagic acid" (no I'd never heard of it either). Any road up, this amazing stuff is rumoured to reduce and even neutralize the damaging effects of carcinogens found in cigarette smoke. This is good news for passive smokers, though I doubt it would have much effect if you are a smoker yourself.

What's best—juice or smoothie?

Strawberry juice is wonderful, but a little pricey and also quite thick. I recommend mixing it with others to thin it down—for instance orange, grapefruit, pineapple, and grape. Strawberries make wonderful additions to almost any smoothie, and once again, like all soft fruits, can be frozen and used all year round. The frozen ones also make beautiful additions to ice cream smoothies (see page 230).

Buying and preparation

When buying any berries you want the freshest you can get; if you can take a day out and go picking in the summer, you can always freeze what you don't use and have them all year round. Early summer is a good time, that's when you know the fruits are at their juiciest, freshest, sun-ripened best. Keep loosely in a brown paper bag (open) in the fridge for a few days. To prepare them, simply take off the little green cap, rinse if they're a little dirty, and either juice or blend.

Tangerines
(and Satsumas, Clementines, and Mandarins)

Over 90 percent delicious, sweet-tasting, body-cleansing water

So before we start, what exactly is the difference between a tangerine, a satsuma, a clementine, and a mandarin? Well to be fair, there isn't a whole heap of difference. They all are members of the same family, the *Rutaceae,* or orange, family. They all taste sweet, look more or less the same, taste kind of similar, and they all make about the same amount of juice. The biggest difference is how easy they are to peel. Mandarins—that's the smaller type with skin that sticks to the fruit like glue—are a pain. They obviously drove clergyman Pierre Clement crazy too. He crossed a mandarin and an orange and came up with a mandarin that was very easy to peel.

Gifts from the Orient

However, "loose-skinned mandarin" was a little bit of a mouthful so they renamed it the clementine. Tangerines are simply orange-red mandarins with a particular citrus taste; again these have loose skin so are easy to peel. The satsuma is also a crossbreed, and these too have a fairly loose skin.

When tangerines, or any other similar loose-skinned, easy-to-peel fruits, are in season, I sometimes choose them over oranges. This is purely a time and mess issue, as it's a lot easier, quicker, and cleaner to peel a tangerine than it is to peel an orange. In order to get orange juice you need to peel it with a knife, keep the "pith on" and then juice it. With these babies you just peel them by hand, throw them in your juicer, and you have instant, mouth-watering juice. The taste, however, is very different to that of oranges (not as tart), and you may well prefer to use both during the summer months.

The Ugly Ugli Fruit

Ever heard of this one—an Ugli fruit? Well, I've included it here because it's a member of the same family as the above. The Ugli fruit is a tangelo, a hybrid of tangerine and grapefruit, and it is very aptly named, as it really does look ugly. However, beauty comes from within and along with its relatives, these babies contain plenty of vitamins (especially C) and minerals to keep your hair shining, your eyes bright, and your immune system strong.

What's best — juice or smoothie?

Juice, juice, juice, juice! When it comes to all citrus fruits, the rule is juice them or eat them. The exception to this is pineapple, which can be used in smoothies as well as juiced. The juice of all citrus fruits can be used as good bases for smoothies.

Buying and preparation

Look for loose-skinned fruits that look fresh and, where possible, buy organic. Preparation couldn't be easier, simply peel by hand, put in the machine and juice. The juice can also be added to a blender with soft fruits to make beautiful smoothies.

Vegetable Fruits

I have put vegetable fruits in their own category. Vegetable fruits are in reality fruits, as any plant bearing food with a seed is technically a fruit. A fruit is actually the edible part of the plant that contains the seeds, while a vegetable is the edible root, leaves, and stems of the plant. Most people think of the following as a type of vegetable and, in a sense, they are. Vegetable fruits such as cucumbers, tomatoes, peppers, and avocados mix very well with vegetable juices, unlike many standard fruits. Juice and enjoy!

Avocado

Surprisingly over 80 percent water

Let's Avo Standing Ovation for the Fat King!

Make no mistake, avocados are king—but not for juicing. So why, you may ask, include them in a juice book? Well although you can't actually juice them, they do blend very well with vegetable juices—much in the same way as bananas blend well with fruit juices. Besides, there was just no way I could do an A–Z of fruit and veg and leave out the undisputed heavyweight champion of the fruit and veg world—avocado.

Nature's Heavyweight but You Won't Gain Weight

Avocados, like bananas, have received some very bad press over the years. However, I would like you to forget what you have read or heard in the past and feast your eyes on the following statement.

avocados will not make you fat
avocados do not contain cholesterol

Never has one food been so misunderstood. It's a good thing nature can't sue for libel or every diet club and a good percentage of diet experts would be in the dock! Avocados are full of fat; yep, that's a fact, but if you have read *Slim 4 Life* you will know that the main type of fat found in avocado is an essential fat—one that the body needs and utilizes. If you ate twenty avocados a day and never moved from your sofa, then perhaps you would put on weight—but if you stuffed your face with anything and never moved you would pile on the pounds.

It's important to bear in mind that cholesterol cannot be found in the plant kingdom; you will only find it in the animal kingdom. Now, unless you have seen an avocado darting around your garden with big eyes, a nose, and a mouth, then I wouldn't worry too much.

If you have avoided avocados because you thought they were fattening or would lead to a cholesterol problem, it's time to get reunited with what is probably the best food in the world.

The One and Only "Complete" Food

All fruit and veg contain amazing life-giving nutrients, but avocados contain virtually the lot. This is why I eat loads of these creamy, almost buttery flavored vegetable fruits daily. It's also why I use them to make the most amazing vegetable smoothies in the world—The Juice Master Complete (page 194) and The Anthony Robbins (page 199). It has been said that avocados are the only complete food on the planet—meaning you could live on these and these alone. Now I don't know if that's true, as living on nothing but avocados would be about as much fun as yanking out your nasal hairs with curling tongs, but they certainly contain all of our six human needs in abundance— water, fat, protein, natural sugar, vitamins, and minerals.

What's best—juice or smoothie?
As mentioned above, avocados do not juice but do blend well with vegetable juices.

Buying and preparation
I only got into avocados a few years back when I changed my eating habits. Prior to that I used to see people in supermarkets squeezing avocados and wondered if they all belonged to some kind of cult— now I understand what they were up to. When buying avocados, look for ones that are heavy for their size and are free of bruises and dark sunken spots. If you want to use them the same day or within a few days, then they should be reasonably soft when you squeeze them. If you can't squeeze them, they are not ripe. Place them in a brown bag at room temperature for a few days and you will soon have fully ripe avocados. To prepare them, cut in half, take out the big seed (this

should more or less fall out when ripe) and spoon out the flesh. Put in the blender, add some juice (carrot, celery, cucumber, lemon, and the like), mix and enjoy.

JM TIP—Always add lemon juice to vegetable smoothies made with avocado; it helps to slow down the rate of oxidation.

Cucumbers

Over 95 percent cool, refreshing, life-enhancing water

As Cool as a Cucumber

Wow, wow, wow again! The expression "cool as a cucumber" couldn't be more apt, for the humble cucumber is one of nature's most cooling, refreshing, versatile, cleansing, and high-juice-yielding veggie fruits. The famous expression isn't the only thing that holds water: it is also quite simply the water champ of the vegetable juice world. As such, its ability to cool the inner body is right up there with watermelon and celery. Cucumbers maintain a cool inside temperature on a hot day; this is why in many hot countries you will see cucumber on the menu virtually wherever you go—they are nature's natural coolants.

Is It All Hair-Say?

It has been claimed that cucumber juice has the ability to rejuvenate muscles, give elasticity to skin—even promote hair and fingernail growth and prevent hair loss. Cucumbers are also perhaps the best natural diuretic known to wo/man kind and are just magnificent for skin problems. On top of that, they contain lots of those handy bioflavinoids.

When I make a vegetable juice of any kind, nine times out of ten it will include cucumber. This is not only because it is great value (the high water content means it goes a long way) but it is also an invaluable aid to supreme health. The cucumber really is one food that you should have on your "must eat" list every day. The difference to your health and well-being, over a period of time, will be quite amazing. And even if you don't get round to juicing them, there are many things that people have done with cucumbers that have been very beneficial that don't involve eating or juicing them (Steady!). Yep, they're even great for cooling and rejuvenating tired eyes—simply slice and place over the eyes (while lying down, naturally!).

What's best—juice or smoothie?

Once again—juice. You can, however, chop them, put them into a blender, add another vegetable juice, and make a type of vegetable smoothie (see page 193).

Buying and preparation

Look for firmness and a dark skin. If the cucumbers are waxed you may want to peel before juicing, although most of the pesticides, waxes, and such will end up in the pulp and not the juice. I tend to juice organic cucumbers where possible.

Peppers

Over 85 percent nutrient-packed water

We're talking bell peppers here—so called because of their shape— not sure where the pepper part came from

 I simply love peppers and will use them to jazz up all kinds of salads, stir fries, and pasta dishes. However, the juice of these amazing vegetable fruits is even more delicious, and because the body doesn't have to spend tons of energy trying to squeeze the juice from the fibers—and because you don't apply heat—it's even better for your health, your energy levels, your immune system and your longevity.

From the Nightshade Family

Peppers come in many tantalizing colours—green, red, yellow, orange, and even black. However, they all start life the same color—green. The different colors are simply different stages of ripeness. Peppers do not continue to ripen once they've been picked; this is why the colored varieties have oodles more nutrients than the green type—they have ripened on the vine and as such are superior to the unripe green ones. That is not to say that the green ones aren't worth juicing, they are—in fact one raw pepper, even the green kind, has more vitamin C than a cup of orange juice.

The juice from peppers, although mild-tasting, is pretty potent, so it should always be mixed with other juices such as carrot, apple or cucumber. The late great Dr. Norman Walker was a huge fan of green pepper juice—he particularly liked the abundance of silicon found in this juice, which is great for your hair and nails.

What's best—juice or smoothie?
Definitely juice. You will get the most benefit from these little beauties by either drinking their fine juice or from chopping them up and putting them into a fab salad. Having said that, you can chop them up into small chunks and put them in the blender; add some carrot, apple, cucumber, beetroot, and celery juice; a bit of ginger; blend; and boom—you have live nutrition in a glass. I tend to just juice them but hey, feel free to do what you like.

Buying and preparation
Choose peppers that have a good color but are not too glossy. If they're too shiny it's usually a sign of waxing on the fruit—try to avoid these where possible. Peppers should be firm and feel heavy for their size. Whole, fresh, unwashed green peppers will keep in the refrigerator for

three to four days. Since colored peppers are riper than green ones, they will spoil faster, so use them within one to two days.

To prepare them for juicing simply give them a quick rinse, cut into small enough chunks to fit in the chute of your juicing machine (if you've got a good machine they fit in just as they are), and juice the lot—yep everything, including the seeds.

Tomatoes

Over 85 percent nutrient rich water

The Anchovy of the Fruit and Veg World

 I must say without these truly vibrant super-foods, salads just wouldn't be the same. I personally love tomatoes and will add them to any wholemeal pasta or salad dish. However, I really am not that keen on the juice. I know that may sound somewhat odd coming from The Juice Master, but tomato juice is a bit like anchovies—you either love it or hate it. I fall into the latter camp, although I find it OK mixed with some other juices. You, of course, may love it. While I was writing this book I got a load of friends round to try the recipes, and many of them thought the tomato juice ones were the best.

Pure Natural Med-ication

Tomatoes have had plenty of good publicity over the years and for good reason. Study after study has shown that tomatoes have incredible cancer-fighting agents, in particular one called lycopenes. Lycopenes are part of the family of pigments called carotenoids, which are natural compounds that give fruits and vegetables their color. Beta-carotene, for example, is the orange pigment in carrots. I've already mentioned on numerous occasions the antioxidant properties of beta-carotene. However, in lab tests lycopene was found to be twice as powerful as beta-carotene at neutralizing free radicals. If that's sounding all a bit blah, blah, blah to you, think about places where tomatoes are eaten as part of the *everyday* diet, for instance in the Med. In these areas the number of people suffering from all cancers is significantly lower than in northern European countries. Now of course there are many contributing factors, like beautiful sunshine and fresh air, but there is no question that these little red babies are bursting with more nutrients than you can chuck a bottle of ketchup at and, unquestionably, play an important role in keeping the body free from disease.

What's best—juice or smoothie?
No question—juice.

Buying and preparation
When buying, look for firm, deep red tomatoes, preferably organic or at least spray-free. To prepare for juicing, simply chop to the size of the chute on your machine, juice, and enjoy.

Vegetables

GET THE BASE RIGHT

There is one fruit juice that mixes particularly well with vegetables—apple (pineapple is pretty good too), and thank God it does. Most vegetable juices taste, well, how can I put it . . . earthy. I have been juicing for so long and my taste buds have changed so much that I actually like the earthy taste. However, those who have just started juicing may not find it very pleasant. The neat way to get round this is simply by using "crapple" juice. A crapple juice is a mixture of apple and carrot—two-thirds carrot, one-third apple. This delicious, sweet-tasting combination should make up 50–75 percent of your vegetable juice. You can then add the more potent and powerful juices (the "earthy" tasting ones) to make up the remainder—spinach, beetroot, asparagus, broccoli, and so on.

Another option is to add pineapple juice to carrot instead of apple. This is known as "Crapineapple" juice. Because carrot juice is sooooo sweet and yummy, you can skip the apple/pineapple and just have carrot as your base if you prefer, making the whole thing pure vegetable juice. As you get used to the taste, start including cucumber and, if you like it, celery juice as part of the base. Ideally a vegetable juice is made up of 50 percent carrot, crapple, or crapineapple and 25 percent cucumber and celery—other vegetables then make up the remaining 25 percent. You will see that many of my vegetable juice recipes have a crapple or carrot base, and if you stick to this base when making your own concoctions you can't really go wrong.

Another tip for great-tasting juice is to juice half a lemon or lime and add that to the base—the difference can be quite incredible.

Unlike fruits and some vegetable fruits, vegetables do not blend to make smoothies. The only time vegetables blend well is when making homemade soups (with the exception of avocado). Therefore vegetables should always be juiced (or eaten obviously).

There are a couple of things I want to repeat, as they are important—I tend to *eat* most of my fruit and *drink* most of my veg. This doesn't mean I never have delicious fruit juices and smoothies, because I do and I love 'em! It's just that I also love *eating* raw fruit and so tend to get my fiber that way, but I'm not as keen to dive into a plate of raw broccoli and carrots at the end of the day. Therefore I tend to have one fruit juice or smoothie a day (usually in the morning) and two lots of heavenly vegetable juice.

Those of you who are vegetable juice "virgins" may think the words heavenly and vegetable juice should never be put in the same sentence, but you'd be wrong. Follow the guidelines set out below and your vegetable juices will taste fab every time.

Asparagus

What's Cooking Good Looking?

I must say when it comes to eating this popular vegetable starter, I've never really been a fan. But, as I always say, if you really can't eat a particular veg that you know will do you oodles of good—then drink it. That's why I love juicing so much; even if you don't like a particular veg you can juice it, mix it with a few other juices, and you get all the goodness in a way that tastes great. In fact, you get much, much more goodness because the body doesn't have to use energy trying to separate the juices from the fibers and, more importantly, it stays raw.

When you cook any live food you kill many of the nutrients. In the case of asparagus you kill the single most valuable nutrient contained within it, an alkaloid called asparagines. This stuff does wonders—it stimulates the kidneys, works a powerful diuretic, purifies the blood, and helps the bowels. Asparagus also contains bioflavinoids.

Rumor-tism

The late, great Dr. Norman Walker was a huge fan of this juice and spoke about its amazing ability to break up the oxalic acid crystals, making it excellent for rheumatism. But whatever you do, like all "green" juices, don't drink this juice by the gallon or by itself—green juices are potent and should always be mixed with other juices such as carrot, apple, cucumber, and such. Just because one juice is perhaps more beneficial for one particular ailment, doesn't mean flooding your system with it increases the benefit, in fact the opposite is true. What you are looking for is a holistic, balanced approach to your diet, and including the juice of this wonderful vegetable will certainly help.

Buying and preparation

As you may already be aware, this stuff isn't cheap (due to labor-intensive cultivation costs)—so it's a good thing you don't need that much. This green juice is potent and is a must to drink it with other juices, so stick to the base rule (page 85). When buying you can go for either the thin or thick variety, both are excellent. They should be bright green with tight tips. Preparation is simple—just put the whole thing through the juicer, mix with other veg juices, and enjoy.

Beet

You Just Can't Bloody Beet It

 Raw beet is about as appealing as a holiday in Afghanistan, but juice it, mix it with a good base juice, and drink it and you will have furnished your body with one of the very best natural blood builders on the planet. In the words of Dr. Norman Walker, "Beet juice is one of the most valuable juices for helping to build up the red corpuscles of the blood and tone up the blood generally." Beet is also rich in carotenoids, the anticancer king. If all that isn't enough, they also contain plenty of vitamin C and the magnificent mineral manganese—helping brain function, bones, and sugar metabolism.

Pure Nutrition at the Red-dy

From these earthy veg you get a very deep red and potent juice—again not to be drunk by itself (always mix with a base juice and never drink too much, especially if you have sugar problems). The color is so powerful that just the juice of one small beet will turn even the greenest of vegetable juices a beautiful shade of red. When serving vegetable juices containing beetroot with a meal, it's a good idea to pour into large wine glasses. You can then sip your juice with your meal, as you would wine—and of course you'll be getting an amazing supply of powerful enzymes rather than a hangover!

Buying and preparation

When buying beets, look for smooth, firm ones.

Beets should be stored in the fridge or in a cool part of the house. To prepare, simply chop off the stalks, wash, and juice.

Broccoli

Veg Nutrient Power at Its Best

This is where juicing really comes into its own. Vegetables like raw broccoli are not only fairly difficult for the body to digest (and more

importantly to assimilate) but quite frankly are about as tasty as the inside of one of Gandhi's flip-flops! Some people do like raw broccoli, and hats off to them, but they often don't realize it's actually quite hard for the body to absorb the nutrients it contains. Things are much easier for the body when broccoli is lightly steamed, but the problem with this, as you will recall, is that you lose vital live nutrients and enzymes when you apply heat. This doesn't mean that steamed broccoli isn't any good, because it is—very good, in fact. However, to truly get the very best raw broccoli has to offer it needs to be juiced.

Pure Sunshine for Your Cells

Broccoli is worth an absolute mint in terms of abundant health, vitality, and longevity. All fruits and veg are fantastic, but broccoli, like all the green vegetables, is in the premiership. All green veg contain oodles (yes official word) of nutrients, antioxidants, and a substance called chlorophyll. This amazing stuff traps the energy of sunlight within the plant; it is only when the plant is broken down (when it is juiced for instance) that this energy is released. Imagine getting an injection of pure natural sunshine and live nutrients flowing through your cells every day. Well, have any vegetable juice containing this amazing veg and you won't have to imagine it (see The Broccoli Spears page 208).

Simply the Breast

As you will know by now, I'm not a fan of saying that one particular juice, fruit, or veg will help one particular health problem; I'm into the holistic approach—treating the body as a complete unit. After all, if you eat nothing but rubbish and have one glass of juice a week it will be about as useful as a gum shield for Mike Tyson! However, certain fruits or vegetables can offer protection from a particular ill and broccoli is one of them. As well as heaps of calcium, selenium, potassium, and an impressive array of vitamins, broccoli also contains something called indol-3 carbonal. This stuff seems to emulsify estrogen in women and, according to the National Cancer Institute, may reduce the risk of breast cancer. Personally I'm not into the word "may," but there is no question that the body has a much better chance of staying vibrantly healthy when it has live nutrients furnishing its cells.

Buying and preparation

Broccoli should be bright green, have firm stalks, and smell nice and fresh. It's available all year round, but as they are a cool-weather veg they're at their very best between January and March. Preparation couldn't be easier—you can juice every single part, including the stalks. Layer it in between other veg such as carrots and push it through the juicer slowly—that way you extract more of the juice.

Brussels Sprouts

Well I must say that without my cousin's intervention this veg wouldn't have made it into the book (so you can thank one Jodine Thogmartin if this juice helps you and your ills). Personally, I hate Brussels sprouts, always have, and no doubt always will. Although I'm a firm believer that you can train your taste buds to like just anything if you have it on a regular basis, I must say I think the exception to that rule is Brussels sprouts! Now many of you out there will already love this veg, and if you do, I take my hat off to you. For those who don't, help is once again at hand in the form of juice power. Yes, despite the fact I hate *eating* Brussels sprouts, once the juice is mixed with sweeter ones such as apple, carrot, and pineapple, I'm perfectly happy to drink it.

Cancer "Hari-Kari"

When I was a kid my mother was endlessly trying to get me to eat Brussels sprouts. It was a battle she lost all the time, but I now realize she was right to try because these things are just loaded with goodness. Brussels sprouts contain the potent anticancer compound sinigrin, which "persuades" precancerous cells to commit suicide (a natural process called apoptosis)—how neat is that? This action is so powerful that research from the Institute of Food Research in Norwich, England, suggests that even the occasional meal of sprouts can destroy these cells. The amazing health benefits of this sprout don't stop there either, they are a rich source of folate (the food form of folic acid), which is said to help reduce the risk of birth defects if taken prior to pregnancy.

Insulin Regenerator

If you are diabetic, or borderline (as many are) please do yourself a massive favor by first cutting out all concentrated sugars and starches and then getting some Brussels sprout, carrot, string bean, and lettuce juice inside you on a regular basis. This combination of nutritional elements helps to strengthen and regenerate the insulin-generating properties of the pancreas—meaning it can be superb for diabetes. (Of course, if you are still eating loads of white, refined rubbish, then its insulin-regenerating effects will be pretty weak.)

Buying and preparation

The milder the sprout the less it's going to do for you, so buy the most potent you can get. When juicing, just wash and juice.

Cabbage

 Just the word cabbage is usually enough to make anyone run a mile. My first memory of this vegetable was of sitting down at the dinner table being literally forced to eat the limp remains of what started life as fresh raw cabbage. It seems somewhat ironic that a few years later I would voluntarily be boiling the stuff up myself on an infamous "cabbage soup diet". Needless to say, just the smell of cabbage cooking is still enough to make me retch. If I'm so against it, why have I put it in the book? Well I have absolutely nothing against cabbage at all, as long as it's kept out of the pan. Like all of nature's wonderful fuels, some, if not all, of the "live" nutrients are destroyed when you apply heat. To make matters worse, when you eat cooked cabbage what you often end up with is sulphur resting in various pockets of the stomach, causing, how can I put this politely—foul wind! And to think most of us were literally forced to eat this stuff in the name of "health."

A Grate Way to Have It Raw

I must say that when I changed my brand of food, the idea of eating raw cabbage didn't really appeal, but there is a way of eating it raw that is very tasty. Simply grate it. Grated red or white cabbage sprinkled over any salad certainly brightens it up and also adds an amazing flavor. But perhaps the best way to get the raw power from this cruciferous veg is once again to juice it. However, like so many veg, the juice from raw cabbage is well, an acquired taste—in other words it sucks. But, I will repeat again, when it comes to veg you should always mix them with a sweet base of apple or carrot or both mixed—that way you get all the goodness of raw cabbage without having to eat it or even taste it.

Cabbage Juice Therapy

Cabbage is incredibly rich in beta-carotene, folic acid, and vitamin C, and, if grown in mineral-rich soil, selenium. In addition, like so many fruit and veg, it also has amazing healing properties. Cabbage is a good source of the amino acid glutamine—nature's antiulcer king. As far back as the late 1940s, Dr. Garnet Cheney and Jay Kordich demonstrated that cutting junk from the diet and supplying oodles of "fast food" has an amazing affect on stomach ulcers. They conducted an experiment involving sixty-five volunteers with stomach ulcers: all of these patients were given just cabbage, celery, and carrot juice for three weeks, by which time sixty-three out of the sixty-five patients were totally healed and the other two had only minimal symptoms.

Was it the cabbage juice that healed them? The carrot juice? The celery juice? A combination of all three? Who knows, but one thing is certain, freeing the body of the energy-zapping process of digestion while feeding it live nutrients in a liquid form goes a long way to giving the body every possible chance to heal. And because each vegetable and fruit has its own unique protective and healing properties, it's worth adding things like cabbage to your juice every now and then.

Buying and preparation
Look for cabbages that look healthy on the outside; you don't want to have to throw half of it away to get to the fresh stuff underneath. To prepare, cut into pieces small enough to fit the chute and simply juice. Remember to add to other juices such as carrot and apple.

Carrots

Hail the King

 If you have only ever tasted carrot juice from a carton or bottle then you are in for one hell of a creamy treat. Freshly extracted organic carrot juice is amazingly sweet and the creamy texture complete with frothy head is akin to a pint of Guinness. Carrot, like apple, will become one of your best friends in your juice kitchen, as virtually every vegetable juice you make will include it somewhere in the equation—not least because it makes even the most, let's say, "earthy" versions taste sweet and yummy. Carrot juice is one of the only vegetable juices I have by itself and it is also the one that children usually have no problem with because its color and taste are very close to that of fruit juice. Even if the first glass doesn't quite make you want to leap over the moon, you will find it takes just a couple of "workouts" in the taste gym and you'll be loving it. And in terms of your health it's certainly worth getting the taste for. Raw "live" carrot juice is loaded with a host antidisease beauties, including vitamins B, C, D, E, K, folic acid, and the anticancer king, beta-carotene.

The Eyes Have It

As well as an amazing ability to strengthen the immune system and fight cancer cells, carrots also have the incredible power to improve night vision and eyesight in general. According to Dr. Sandra Cabot, author of *Raw Juices Can Save Your Life*, carrots and their wonderful juices also contain an insulin-like compound. This means that although carrot juice is high in natural sugars, small amounts can be used in juice mixtures for diabetics or those with Syndrome X (insulin resistance is a feature of this condition). And if all that isn't enough, Scottish studies have demonstrated that eating just two and a half raw carrots a day can lower cholesterol by 11 percent in just three weeks.

The Mineral Marvel

Carrots also contain potassium, iron, sodium, phosphorus, chromium, magnesium, silica, chlorine, and sulphur. But I will repeat again—it's not how many vitamins or minerals a food contains but how much of it can the body assimilate. This is why juicing vegetables like carrots is just sooooo good. They are loaded with vitamins and minerals galore, but it's hard for the body to extract them from the hard, raw fibers. However, the juice machine does all the work, leaving us with the finest vitamin and mineral supplement on earth in an easy to assimilate, liquid form.

The Man Who Went Orange on Carrot Juice and Died

Carrot juice has received some bad press too—do you remember hearing of a guy who died after drinking too much carrot juice? What they failed to tell you was that as well as drinking eight pints of carrot juice a day, he was also taking mountains of vitamin A tablets—methinks this just might have had something to do with it. So please don't worry about overdosing on carrot juice, carrot juice alone will do you no harm—the only thing that can happen, but you do have to drink a lot of it, is that your skin can indeed change color. I know this firsthand, as it happened to me when I went on my insane "nothing but raw juices for three months" regime some years ago. My skin turned, well—orange! So unless you are fond of orange skin, don't drink more than two to three pints of carrot juice a day. You will probably find that after mixing it with other juices, your total will rarely exceed about a pint anyway.

Buying and preparation

Ideally, go for organic carrots. These need only be rinsed—you don't even need to top and tail them. Having said that, if you don't have a particularly good juicer, it's a good idea to cut the top off, as it can be particularly hard and thus has the ability to wear out the motor on your machine. If, for whatever reason, you can't get hold of organic carrots, then make sure you do top and tail them, as this is where most of the pesticides concentrate, especially in the stem end. However, *do not peel them.* As with most fruits and veg, huge amounts of the nutrients are to be found just under the skin, so just give them a gentle scrub under cold water with a brush. Carrots are best stored in the fridge—they not only keep longer there, but it means you get nice cool juice.

Note: If you are diabetic or worried in any way about sugar levels and insulin, please remember to eat your fruit and drink your veg. Also, make sure that you use no more than 50 percent crapple base and add a little ice.

Cauliflower

"Cabbage with a college education"
Mark Twain

 Cauliflower juice tastes awful, there's just no getting around it, so if you want the benefits of this vegetable you'll need to mix it with some sweet juices such as carrot and apple. I have never been a fan of this particular veg and it's one that I just don't juice or even eat. Having said that, I've put it in, as I know many people who juice this potassium- and phosphorus-rich veg experience amazing results on the health front.

How's This for a Bit of Blah?

As well as vitamins B, C, folic acid, beta-carotene, and the minerals calcium, iron, sulphur, potassium, and phosphorus, cauliflower is also said to contain indol-3 carbonyl, which, as mentioned with broccoli, has been said to help protect women from breast cancer.

Buying and preparation

Look for ivory-colored flesh surrounded by light green leaves—skip any that have any brown bits or florets that seem a bit limp. To prepare for juicing, simply wash, cut to the appropriate size, and juice.

Celery

Salt of the Earth

When it comes to the vegetable world celery is without question the real "salt of the earth." It's a good thing too, as salt is an absolute must for the human body. It's necessary for the generation and function of digestive fluids in the system—without salt good digestion is virtually impossible.

So All Salt Is Good for You Then?
Not Nessa-Celery!

However, the salt we consume must be entirely soluble in water—like that in celery. Table salt is not completely water-soluble and is highly addictive, which is why in the US we go through 145,000 tons of this toxic high-blood-pressure-forming substance every year. While table salt is a man-made substance that can result in hardening of the arteries, celery is a completely natural, rich source of organic sodium.

The Workout King

No Sweat!

Celery juice, combined with apple, will become your best friend during hot weather or if you workout on a regular basis. When we exercise (or play as I prefer to call it), we lose vital nutrients and body fluids through our sweat glands. And what's the best way to replace those nutrients? Yep—celery juice. Mix it with some apple and you've concocted perhaps the single most effective and refreshing recovery aid to exercise on the planet. It furnishes your system with sodium, potassium, iron, calcium, phosphorus, magnesium, and vitamins B and C. Celery juice also helps to flush the body of excessive carbon dioxide, which is excellent if you live in a city or drink fizzy drinks of any kind. On top of that it helps to reduce acidity—superb for certain cases of arthritis

Celery juice, like cucumber and carrot, will become one of the staples in your juice kitchen. You will find that most vegetable juices you make will have celery somewhere in it. Like cucumber, it is also one of the only green juices that can be drunk on its own—having said that, it does require some taste training in the JM taste gym. If you really cannot stomach it, a combination of celery, cucumber, and apple juice not only tastes divine but is one of the finest juices for your mental and physical health.

Buying and preparation
Skip the limp stalks and go for healthy crisp ones with good-looking leaves. To prepare, just juice the whole thing, including the leaves.

Dandelion Greens

Fine and Dandy

 Ummmm—flowers, not sure if I've gone barking mad myself here. Veggies are one thing, but flowers? You'll perhaps be pleased to hear that you don't actually eat the flower—it's the rest of the plant we're interested in. Dandelion greens (the roots and green leaves) can indeed be juiced, and if you have a garden, they're free. However, if you can't pick your own, you will find that most good greengrocers and health stores stock them.

Not to Be Sniffed At

For a flower to make it into this book it has to be good, and boy the juice from this flower is something else. Dandelion greens are not only oozing with potassium, calcium, and sodium, but the liquid gold contained within the green leaves and roots are our richest source of magnesium and iron. All of which means it's a belter for increasing bone density, and vital for strong teeth and the prevention of tooth decay. These flowers are loaded with life-giving nutrients designed to feed every single cell in the body, while helping to lift up the rubbish and flush it from the system. Dandelion juice also has a calming effect on the entire central nervous system and is particularly helpful with such diseases as arthritis—mainly due to its ability to normalize the acid/alkaline balance of the body.

Buying, picking, and preparation

The season for dandelion greens is late spring/early summer, when you can either pick them from your own garden or buy them from your local market or greengrocers.

Make sure you wash them well, then just juice them. If you have a centrifugal juicer, make sure you put the leaves in between some bits of apple or carrot and push through the machine slowly. This way you will squeeze the most out of your greens—this is true for all green veg.

Fennel

 Imagine being able to enjoy the beautiful taste of liquorice without having to load your system with sugar at the same time—well if you add some fennel to your vegetable juice that is precisely what you'll get. Now for some people, liquorice is about as appealing as a night in watching repeats of *Diff'rent Strokes*. For others the taste is akin to an angel crying on your taste buds—or something like that. I personally love the aniseed flavor and it's a wonderful tool for injecting an unusual sweetness to some of the earthy vegetable combinations.

Wait Till They Get No Wind with This One!

Fennel has been described as "celery that has been hit with a mallet"—to me it looks like a set of mini bagpipes. Fennel is indeed from the same family as celery, and some of the life-giving nutrients contained in this odd-looking veg are on par with that of its salty cousin. The juice, however, is much, much sweeter and more aromatic. It not only smells nice, but taken on an empty stomach and mixed with say carrot, celery, and cucumber, it will have you smelling sweeter too. How so? Fennel juice has an amazing calming effect on digestion and reduces intestinal cramps, intestinal gas, flatulence, and bloating.

Once again fennel is a valuable addition to your natural pharmacy. It's high in beta-carotene and vitamins B, C, and E and boasts a large number of minerals, including calcium, potassium, selenium, and zinc. Get hold of organic fennel and, because of the selenium and zinc, you will find it an excellent aid to skin conditions such as psoriasis.

Buying and preparation

Try to buy fennel that still has the leaves on and has no yellowing on the bulb. You can store it in the fridge for up to a week or so. Preparation couldn't be easier—there is none, just juice the lot. Be careful though, the juice is very powerful—you only need a small amount, and make certain you mix it with other juices such as carrot, apple, cucumber, or celery.

Garlic

This One Won't Win You Many Friends

Eat this stuff and your friends will talk about you; drink this stuff and you'll have no friends left to talk about you! It's not just vampires who run a mile when they get a whiff of this incredible natural antibiotic; it's everyone. I exaggerate, obviously, but unless you use garlic correctly in your juice kitchen, you and your juicer will stink of the stuff—so for your own and your friends' sake please follow the JM guidelines for using garlic juice.

The good news is that we, along with vampires, are not the only creatures who run a mile when we get a whiff of this—parasites and germs hate the stuff. Garlic is known as nature's most powerful antibiotic, and it seems its healing properties are so powerful that no nasty is safe when you give your body a good dose of this stuff.

The White Sniffs of Clover

The many benefits to be had from consuming garlic are not to be sniffed at. It can reduce blood pressure, blood clotting, and LDL cholesterol (the bad one); helps prevent stomach cancer; and gives a real boost to your immune system. It helps to thin the blood and can therefore play a part in helping to reduce the chances of heart disease and heart attacks. In addition, it also contains allicin, which not only gives it its very potent smell, but apparently helps destroy fungi and yeast in the body. The fact that it will help prevent any kind of yeast/fungi overgrowth in the body is excellent news for those with candida albicans, thrush, or athlete's foot. However, it's not a miracle-worker. If you are eating tons of bread, refined starches, and sugars on a weekly basis, then a little bit of garlic juice will have about as much chance of destroying the yeast parasites as Woody Allen would have of landing one on Lennox Lewis.

How to Juice Garlic without Losing Your Friends

Firstly, never, ever, ever juice garlic by itself and never drink it by itself—*always* mix it with other vegetable juices (glad that's clear). Unless you are specifically treating a disease of the body and are taking it for immunity and preventive measures, then you really don't need that much. I would say no more than one clove at a time—yes it really is that potent. When you do juice garlic, make sure it's the first thing to go in, then follow it with the other vegetables. Better still, push the cloves into the flesh of other fruits or veg like apples and pineapples. This should stop the juicer reeking of the stuff for days. If you find, however, that all juices thereafter taste of garlic, skip the juicing and simply eat it.

Buying and preparation

Never buy garlic that is soft or has black mildew on the papery skin. Store it at room temperature, not in the fridge. When juicing, simply take off the papery skin and pop in your juicer. As long as you only use one small clove and follow it with other veg, you will hardly taste it and you won't smell of the stuff.

Ginger Root

Come on Baby Juice My Fire!

Ginger has very similar health and healing properties to garlic but with one very noticeable difference—you get to keep your friends. Yes, ginger smells a whole lot sweeter than garlic but still gives a nice taste boost to many a vegetable juice (see Ginger Rogers and Fred A. Pear and The Anne Robin"sun", pages 209 and 197). This doesn't mean it renders garlic obsolete; far from it, garlic is the supreme antibiotic. Ginger is not a replacement for garlic, but realistically you are much more likely to juice ginger than garlic. In fact, I tend to juice garlic once a week at most, yet I use ginger daily—and in terms of health, taste, and variety I'm glad I do.

Something To Shout About

A little bit of ginger goes a long way—a one inch cube mixed with a sweet juice like apple can actually help heal vocal cords if you are having problems finding your voice. Ginger root, like garlic, is a natural antibiotic for the entire body. It is also an amazing mucus and phlegm remover, making it one of nature's supreme decongestants. It's tremendous for travel sickness, inhibits the formation of blood clots, lowers bad cholesterol, and is a natural anti-inflammatory, making it useful for arthritic pain. It won't win any prizes for its vitamin content with only C making a showing, but on the mineral front it has copper, potassium, sodium, iron, calcium, zinc, phosphorus, and magnesium.

Buying and preparation

Ginger root should be plump and firm without any black bits. As with garlic, it should be kept at room temperature—not in the fridge. For juicing, simply cut a smallish piece off and put through the machine. Unlike garlic you don't have to put it through in any particular order for smell reasons, but I've found you get the most out of your ginger if you feed it through in between other pieces of veg.

Parsley

Parsley is generally categorized as an herb, but it can be used just like any other green leafy vegetable—and has just as much nutritional value. However, it makes one hell of a potent juice, so never, ever drink this stuff on its own—always dilute it with other juices such as carrot.

More Than Just a Bit on the Side!

When I was growing up, parsley was always that annoying bit of green stuff on the side of the plate getting in the way of my fish and chips. I now realize that in terms of genuine nutrition, I would have been much better off leaving the fried stuff and getting into the green stuff. Parsley is just so much more than a bit on the side; it's packed with all the vitamins and minerals you'd expect from nature's kitchen, plus oodles of chlorophyll—the green pigment in plants that is effectively the trapped energy of sunlight. When it comes to metabolizing oxygen in the bloodstream and purifying the blood there is simply nothing better than a good shot of chlorophyll, and the often discarded parsley is bursting with the stuff. A shot of parsley juice, diluted with carrot and cucumber juice, is perhaps the closest you will get to being able to inject sunshine into your cells.

Time to Raise Your Glasses
(Without perhaps having to wear them!)

Parsley has other attributes too. According to juice pioneer Dr. Norman Walker, parsley juice, when mixed with carrot or celery and carrot juice, has an even greater healing effect on eyes than carrot alone. In fact, he says "this combination is efficient in every ailment connected with the eyes and optic nerve." So much so that this powerful herb can be used for weak eyes, cataracts, conjunctivitis, and laziness of the pupils.

Now unless you have Green Life, Champion, or similar masticating or twin gear juicer, you may find that unless you juice parsley in the right way you won't get that much juice out of it. So if you own a centrifugal juicer (the most common type) you will need to pack the parsley in the feeder tightly, in between a couple of apples is good, and push through the machine *slowly*—that way you will extract as much juice as is possible.

Buying and preparation
Parsley is very easy to grow in all weathers, so whether you are growing it yourself or buying it, you can be assured of a year-round supply. Look for dark green, either flat or curly parsley with no sign of yellowing. Parsley requires no preparation—but do remember to include the stalks when juicing. To reiterate, if you have a centrifugal juicer you must pack the parsley in firmly while the machine is off and then push it through the juicer slowly. For best extraction, pack it between bits of apple or carrot.

Parsnip

"The garden parsnip . . . is good and wholesome . . . It is good
for the stomach and reins (kidneys) and provoketh urine"
Culpepper (1653)

Parsnip juice—it doesn't sound good does it? And to be fair, compared to most of the others in this book, the therapeutic value isn't the greatest. Having said that, it doesn't mean it's a waste of space—there are many benefits to this sweet-tasting root veg. It is super rich in silicon and sulphur, making it wonderful for brittle nails, while its phosphorus and chlorine content make it wonderful for the lungs and the bronchial system. According to Dr. Norman Walker "The high potassium content is of such excellent value to the brain that this juice has been effectively used in many mental disorders."

Parsnip juice tastes sweet, some say sweeter than carrot, but don't believe them. It does, however, give an added sweetness when combined with other juices.

Buying and preparation

When buying parsnips, look for a firm vegetable. Cut to size of chute and juice the whole thing. Never be tempted to juice the wild variety, as they contain some potentially poisonous ingredients.

Spinach

Popeye Was on to Something!

Veggies have, in the general scheme of things, received a pretty bad press over the years. However, there was one character that did more for green leafy veg, and in particular spinach, than any health campaign ever has—

yep, Popeye. Now I'm not about to suggest that if you eat spinach you'll instantly gain incredible strength, but there is no doubt that spinach is one of nature's most incredible muscle and bone builders.

Eat it daily and you can be sure you are supplying your body with some of the finest tools needed to make much-needed muscle and bone tissue. Spinach contains a substantial amount of protein and in an accessible form that the body can easily assimilate and use. Spinach and its fine juice are also loaded with calcium and vitamin C, both of which work beautifully to keep teeth and gums healthy. Many juice practitioners use a combination of spinach and carrot juice to successfully treat bleeding gums and pyorrhea (a very mild form of scurvy), which are usually the direct result of years of eating refined sugars and starches.

Any Old Iron

Spinach is perhaps most famous for its iron content—the anemia-blasting liquid in its leaves is one of the best sources of iron in the world. Raw spinach is also one of the best cleansers and regenerators for the intestinal tract, which helps to keep us moving (if you know what I mean).

> **"In raw spinach, nature has furnished man with the finest organic material for the cleansing, reconstruction and regeneration of the intestinal tract"**
> Dr. Norman Walker

Its ability to repair the intestinal wall also helps tremendously with skin conditions such as psoriasis and eczema. In addition, spinach helps to stimulate blood circulation, and liver and lymph glands, and has also been used in the treatment of arthritic pain. All in all, it's an absolute must for your "fast-food" kitchen.

Buying and preparation
Your budget and the type of juicing machine you have will determine

what sort of spinach you buy. For example, organic baby leaf spinach is very expensive, so I would strongly advise eating this kind of spinach. Don't forget, eating raw spinach is wonderful—it tastes good and is very easy for the body to break down and assimilate. The spinach I tend to juice is from the big special offer bags in supermarkets, or loose from the market. Organic and "spray-free" are clearly better, but if you cannot get hold of them bear in mind that as long as you wash the leaves to remove some of the chemicals, the spinach is still oozing with goodness.

The way in which you juice spinach is very important, especially if you own a standard centrifugal juice extractor. Always pack spinach in the feeder tightly while the machine is off, then put it through the juicer slowly. That way you will extract as much juice as possible from its leaves. If you own a Green Life juicer, or similar, there is no need to do this—simply feed as you go.

Turnip

Dem Bones Dem Bones Dem Strong Bones!

 There just isn't a vegetable on the planet that can beat the turnip for its incredible calcium content—it's simply loaded with the finest bone-strengthening mineral known to wo/man kind. If you have any kind of softening of the bones, including your teeth, then I strongly recommend getting some of this super fluid circulating in your body. Combine turnip juice with carrot and dandelion green juice and you have one of the most effective substances for hardening the teeth and bones (see Turnip, Turnip, Turnip page 214).

The main concentration of calcium is to be found in the turnip tops, so make sure you buy the complete turnip and juice the whole thing to get maximum benefit. The raw tops also contain an unbelievable concentration of vitamin C—twice as much as oranges—and also have vitamins B, C, E, and good old cancer-bashing beta-carotene. On the mineral front, turnip also contains iron, phosphorus, and potassium. There is, however, a down side. The taste of turnip juice is, well, pretty bitter—so make sure you mix it with sweet juices such as apple and carrot. If you have a chesty cough or bronchitis, mix the juice of a lemon with some turnip juice—it may taste like a wet weekend in New Jersey, but it will have you fighting fit in no time.

Let's Get to the Bottom of the Problem

Hemorrhoids—does this word mean anything to you? I sincerely hope not, for they sound like a right royal pain in the butt. Many of the junk foods we consume contain calcium—"that's good" I hear you cry; well not really. The problem is this type of calcium is "inorganic"—this means the cells and tissues of the body cannot use it for constructive purposes. This in turn means the blood must shift these inorganic substances out of the way into the ends of blood vessels—and the most convenient of these are found . . . in your rectum. However, help is at hand to the half of you (yep that many) who have this problem—two pints of turnip juice, with equal amounts of watercress, spinach, and carrot drank daily will help to shift all the built-up mess in just a month (in conjunction with a healthy diet and plenty of raw fruit and vegetables).

Buying and preparation
Try to buy turnips that still have the leaves attached, as the combination of root and leaf maximizes the calcium content. Juice everything to make sure you get all the nutrient power of this, the calcium king of the vegetable world.

Watercress

The Sulphur King

 Not all juice extractors are designed with watercress in mind, but like spinach, as long as you pack it into the chute while the machine is turned off and then push it through slowly, you will get the maximum amount of juice your machine will allow. Now if that doesn't look like much, don't despair, as watercress juice is pretty powerful and a little goes a long way. Like all green juices, with the exception of cucumber and celery, watercress juice should never be drunk by itself; *always* dilute it with other juices or even just mineral water.

Watercress juice is extremely rich in sulphur and iron and, combined with turnip, carrot, and spinach juice (in equal parts) is good for anemia and helps to dissolve coagulated blood in piles—lovely! Watercress is also loaded with calcium, carotene, and vitamin C.

Buying and preparation

Watercress used to be a common sight growing at the edge of pure, slowly running water. Unfortunately, pollution and commercial factors have meant the chances are you will now have to buy it. If you buy it loose, make sure you store it lightly wrapped in a plastic bag in the fridge. To juice, simply pack tight into the chute of your juice machine while it's turned off and then push through slowly with other produce once it's on.

Wheatgrass

Make Mine a Shot of Sunshine

 OK, so now you think I've finally lost it—I talk about "nutrition for reality" and yet here I am putting grass in a juice book, why? Well, I've included it simply because the incredible nutritional and healing power of freshly extracted wheatgrass juice cannot be ignored.

Wheatgrass is described by many in the "raw food" world as a "superfood." This is mainly due to what can only be described as its miraculous effect on terminal illnesses. Dr. Anne Wigmore is perhaps the most famous pioneer of wheatgrass juice, and her amazing work nourishing terminally ill patients back to health with wheatgrass juice at her Hippocrates Health Institute in Boston is well documented. The "live"

supercharged nutrients are so concentrated that Anne Wigmore reported 15 pounds of wheatgrass contains the nutritional equivalent of 350 pounds of other green vegetables.

Look at the Stats

Just a one-ounce shot of wheatgrass juice is packed with more bioflavinoids and phytonutrients than you can shake a Flymo at! It has buckets of enzymes, an amazing amount of antioxidants, twenty amino acids (the building blocks for protein), and a truly remarkable lineup of vitamins and minerals—including vitamins B, C, E, K, folic acid, B17, and beta-carotene, calcium, zinc, selenium, magnesium, phosphorus, manganese, potassium, sodium, sulphur, and cobalt. On top of that it is one of the richest sources of chlorophyll on the planet. The famous research scientist E. Bircher described chlorophyll as "concentrated sunshine." This liquid sunshine improves the functioning of the heart, the vascular system, the intestines, the uterus, and the lungs; it cleans and detoxifies blood and liver; helps to strengthen the immune system; and reduces high blood pressure—pretty impressive stuff.

But It's Grass—That Just Can't Be Natural

In a way, we have been juicing grass since the dawn of time; only the machine used was not an electric one, but simply our mouth. It is clear that it is completely unnatural for humans to eat grass—the strong cellulose makes it too woody and fibrous for our intestinal tract to deal with efficiently. However, one of our most instinctive acts as children is to pick blades of grass and suck on them, and this, as I've since found out, is incredibly good for ulcers, teeth, and gums.

If you are not convinced and think you would rather staple your tongue to the desk than drink grass juice—then skip it. Wheatgrass juice is a good nutrition tool if you want to use it, but *if* you don't, you will get all the nutrients you will ever need from the fruit and veg already listed. Having said that, if you are treating any kind of illness, a shot of wheatgrass juice should certainly be on the health menu daily—it is such a concentrated form of supercharged nutrients that I think it's a must in such situations.

Small Shot or a Mix?

There are a couple of ways people drink wheatgrass juice; one is to have it by itself in a very small dose. Ever walked into one of those hip and trendy health bars and seen people having "shots" of wheatgrass juice? These are the people who've heard that doing shots of wheatgrass juice is this year's black! I personally ask for my wheatgrass juice to be mixed with other sweeter juices, like carrot for example. There is a very good reason for this—wheatgrass juice by itself, like most green juices, tastes like a wet weekend in Halifax. Many do claim they feel "supercharged" after having a shot and good luck to 'em. I just cannot stomach it by the shot, but if you can, feel free.

Bottoms Up!

I read recently that there is one other way to get the therapeutic benefits of wheatgrass juice without actually having to drink it. How? I wish I was joking, but it is suggested "it can be applied rectally using an enema implant" or, in layman's terms—you shove a pipe up your bottom and pump it in! Now call me Mr. Unadventurous, but NO CHANCE. The whole drinking grass thing is debatable enough, but if you feel inclined to shove it up your bum I reckon you should be considering seeing a shrink ASAP.

Buying, preparation, and growing

As you might expect, buying wheatgrass is not that easy unless you live in one of the major cities. If you don't, it is a piece of cake to grow yourself. Wheatgrass growing kits are available from several online sites such as Products for Health (www.productsforhealth.com).

There is a good chance you will also need a separate wheatgrass juice extractor. Centrifugal juicers are just not designed for the job. You will either need a Green Star 1000, a Visor, or some other kind of masticating juice machine. However, these machines are expensive and you probably won't want to invest in one if you have already have a good centrifugal juicer. In this case, there is a handy manual machine that does the job for around £75.

15

Recipes

Let's Get Fruity

The Dixie Kicks

**Very tasteful, extremely thick, and blends well together.
Gives you one hell of a *kick* like a Texas Bronco!**

You will need (loads of talent/nude magazine cover, a president from a different state—sorry I mean . . .)

- 2 apricots
- ½ a banana
- Cinnamon
- 6 pears
- 2 large oranges for a bit of twang
- And it's got to be worth a mint so 6 leaves!

What you do with it
Destone the apricots and place in blender along with ½ a banana, a pinch of cinnamon and the mint leaves. Juice the pears and oranges (make sure you leave as much pith on the oranges as possible when you peel them). Pour into the blender and harmonize for 45 seconds.

Serves 1–2 (1 large glass or 2 medium)

The Jack Lemon

**A cut above the zest and
a total plum!**

You will need (A slobby room mate, a grumpy old man, hold the wine
and roses, sorry I mean . . .)

- 1 lemon (no sorry make that ½ a lemon)
- 1 plum
- ½ a lime
- 4 oranges
- The odd couple of pears (2 conference)
- Handful of ice
- Some cinnamon

What you do with it

Leave the peel on the ½ lemon and lime but peel the oranges. Seed
the plum and place in a blender. Juice the lemon, lime, oranges, and
pears then add to the plums, along with the ice and cinnamon. Blend
the lot for 45 seconds.

Serves 1–2

What a Pithy

A very "simple" one but ith's a winner!

You will need

- 1 small pink grapefruit, or half a large (with plenty of the pith left on)
- 4 oranges (with plenty of pith again)
- ½ a pineapple
- Some ice

What you do with it

Peel the grapefruit and oranges carefully with a sharp knife, making sure you keep as much pith on as possible (remember, the highest concentrate of vitamins and minerals are to be found right next to the skin, so it's very important to keep as much pith on as you can). Cut the piece of pineapple in half and peel the skin off as thinly as possible. (If you are using an organic pineapple, there's no need to peel it). Juice the lot, mix with a spoon, add ice, and enjoy.

Serves 1–2

The "Gorge" Michael

**Best to "go outside" for this one, but be careful who
you offer your juice to!**

You will need

- 1 banana (well come on!)
- 2 apricots (I know!)
- Small handful of fresh or frozen raspberries
- Large handful of fresh or frozen blueberries
- 5 conference pears
- Good handful . . . of ice!

What you do with it

Go to the park and find someone who is only too "policed" to help
you with making your juice—then go home and do the following:

Peel the banana, stone the apricots, and place into blender along
with raspberries, blueberries, and ice. Juice the pears and add to the
blender. Blend everything for 45 seconds and enjoy.

Serves 1–2

"Fig" Brother

A real vote winner!

You will need (No life! Sorry I mean . . .)

- 1 pineapple
- 2 frigs (sorry I mean figs!)
- 1 lemon (there's always one in there somewhere—
  actually make it ½ a lemon)
- 1 plum (there's always a plum too)
- Loads of nuts (Well you've got to be to even want to be in fig brother—
  small handful of almonds)
- Good handful . . . of ice

What you do with it

Strip off the skin from the pineapple (unless it's organic) and figs, making sure you pretend not to know that there are 5 million people watching when exposing naked flesh, and juice with the lemon. Stone the plum and place in the blender with the pineapple and fig juice, nuts and ice. Now simply stare at the blender for hours on end whilst absolutely nothing happens. Eventually, turn it on and hope that you will see some juicy action, perhaps all will blend together to give a taste buds orgy of delight. Any problems please come to the diary room, where we will simply humiliate you as much as possible! Blend for 45 seconds.

You may vote off any of the fruit mates, but if you want "fig" brother to be a winner—use the lot!

Serves 1–2

The Nicool Kidman

**This ice-cool beauty has been designed to satisfy you all
the way down to the very beautiful legs . . . er, dregs!
"To die for"**

You will need (Several juicy roles, as many hairstyles, a Cruise that
goes wrong—sorry I mean . . .)

1 real peach
🍓 4 apricots
🍓 Handful of ice
🍓 1 kiwi (OK I know, but there's no such fruit as an "Aussie" so it's the closest
🍓   thing)
4 juicy pears
🍓 ½ a pineapple
🍓

What you do with it
Stone the peach and apricots and put in blender along with the ice
and peeled kiwi. Juice the pears and peeled pineapple and pour into
the blender. Blend for 45 seconds, pour, and enjoy with eyes wide
shut.

Serves 1–2

Pineapple American Idol

Be your own judge of this one!

There was going to be a Simon Cowell Smoothie, but it was, well, quite frankly, decidedly average! Sorry Simon, keep your trousers up . . . oh sorry, I mean chin!

You will need (10,000 wannabes, 9,990 suspect voices, 1 slimy judge, 1 UK judge, and 1 judge who doesn't care if they shatter your confidence for life—sorry I mean . . .)

🍓 1 large pineapple
🍓 Cool medium glass of sparkling mineral water (Perrier)

What you do with it
Top and tail the pineapple and the cut skin off (if you have an organic pineapple just wash, no need to peel). Simply juice the lot and add mineral water.

Serves 1, maybe 2 if you're lucky

Planet of the Grapes

A gorgeous juice—one to go ape over

You will need

- Handful of seeded white grapes
- Handful of seeded black grapes
- Handful of seeded red grapes
- Glass of water (not tap water)
- Handful of ice

What you do with it

Wash the grapes, put in the juicer and juice the lot. Add water and ice and enjoy. To turn this recipe into a healthy spritzer, you can use sparkling water.

NOTE: If you are diabetic or having problems with blood sugar then **do not be tempted to leave out the water and ice**, as grapes are high in glucose (the type of sugar that goes straight into the bloodstream) and in a juice there is no fiber to slow down the absorption of sugar into the bloodstream.

JM TIP: Make sure you keep the grapes in the fridge before juicing, if they are warm add ice to cool.

Serves 1–2

The Bill Gates

An extremely rich smoothie that helps furnish your bank account of life, enables you to truly excel, and makes you feel like a trillion dollars

You will need

- ½ a pineapple
- ¼ handful of gooseberries
- 3 strawberries
- ¼ a banana
- ¼ handful of blueberrles
- 1 kiwi fruit
- 1 peach
- Handful of ice and small glass of mineral water

Takes a bit of time but if you have a window of opportunity (say 98, 2000, or XP) then it's well worth the time invested!

What you do with it all

Juice the pineapple and pour into a blender with all other ingredients. Blend until rich and smooth!

JM TIP: If it's too thick, add more water and/or ice.

Serves 1–2

The Sting

A super cool, extremely rich smoothie, with a little buzz!
Feels of (liquid) gold

You will need

- 4 conference pears
- 2 oranges
- ½ a lime
- ½ a lemon
- ½ a banana
- 1 spoonful of Manuka Active Honey
- 1 handful of ice

What you do with it all

Peel the oranges, lemon, lime (remembering to leave as much of the pith on as possible), and banana. Juice the oranges, lemon, and lime. Place the banana, ice, honey, and juice in a blender. Blend for 45 seconds. Once done, "take that" wonderful Sting juice and let it gently sing on your taste buds—with every breath you take.

Cherry Springer

Go Cherry, Go Cherry, Go Cherry!
Talk to the health 'cos the disease ain't listenin'!

You will need (an audience who have all had successful intelligence and personality bypass operations, loads of burly bouncers who are as thick as whale omelettes, an insincere host, sorry I mean . . .)

- 2 large handfuls of cherries
- Tall glass sparkling spring water
- 1 handful of ice

What you do with it
Seed the cherries. Juice half of them and pour into blender. Add remaining cherries, water, and ice. Blend, pour, whoop, cheer, and yell in true Springer style, for you have created true live entertainment for your cells!

Serves 1

The Ms. Lewinsky

A high-protein drink—with nuts of course!
Nothing goes down as good as this, but watch your clothes –
it could stain

You will need (a good lawyer, sorry I mean . . .)

- 2 plums (I know)
- 1 banana (stop it)
- 1 coconut (it gets worse trust me)
- Handful of nuts (make that ½ a handful of almonds)
- A good juicing pear (well 4 of the conference variety)
- Ice, ice baby

What you do with it

Seed the plums and put in the blender with the banana and almonds. Using a corkscrew, drill a hole in the softest of the three dimples in the coconut and pour the milk into the blender. Juice the pears (take stems off first) and add to the blender. Blend all ingredients until smooth, drink and enjoy.

Serves 1–2

U.S. Election Special 2000

Packs a punch

You will need

🍓 4 peaches
🍓 4 Florida oranges
🍓 ½ a Florida grapefruit
🍓 6 ice cubes

What you do with it

Stone peaches and place in the blender. Take them out and count them again just to make sure you have the correct number. Put back in and immediately seek an injunction to prevent them being recounted. Once the injunction has been turned down, count them again and place back in blender. Now count the oranges until you are blue in the face and then take the skin off—in other words reject the ap-*peel* (sorry—yes I know that was bad). Do the same with the grapefruit. Juice the oranges and grapefruit and pour into the blender. Add ice, blend, pour, drink, and enjoy.

Serves 1–2

The Hugh Hefner

An old concoction but still with plenty of zest!

You will need (a mansion, loads of naked women, an airbrush—sorry I mean . . .)

- A real plum (well 2 actually)
- Passion (1 of the fruit kind)
- Nuts (6 almonds)
- 1 banana
- Small handful of ice
- 1 glass sparkling spring water
- 1 lime
- 4 oranges
- And unlike the real thing—no cheese cake!

What you do with it

Seed and chop the plums and scoop out the flesh from the passion fruit. Put both in a blender along with the almonds, banana, ice and spring water. Juice the lime and oranges and pour into the blender. Blend the lot for 45 seconds, for more passion than you can throw a bunny at.

Serves 2–3

The Caribbean Dream

**This Rolls Royce of smoothies is pure tropical sunshine
for your cells**

You will need (quite a lot of money—this is a real treat but soooooo worth it!)

- 🍓 1 coconut
- 🍓 ¼–½ a medium-sized mango
- 🍓 ½ a papaya
- 🍓 1 banana
- 🍓 1 handful of ice (or small cup of cold mineral water)
- 🍓 1 medium pineapple
- 🍓 3–4 oranges or ½ a grapefruit (your choice)

What you do with it

Drill a hole with a bottle opener in one of the three dimples and pour fresh coconut milk into the blender. Add mango chunks, papaya, banana, and ice/water. Juice the pineapple and oranges/grapefruit. Pour juice into the blender and blend until smooth for heaven in a glass.

NOTE: The white flesh of the coconut can then be eaten with it if you wish (although it's a real bugger to get it out I can tell ya).

Serves 2–4

The Berry Maguire

"Show me the honey!"

You will need

- 1 good handful of fresh or frozen blackberries
- 1 good handful of fresh strawberries (replace with frozen raspberries if needed)
- 1 handful of fresh or frozen blueberries
- 5 oranges
- ½ cup of mineral water
- Small handful of ice
- 1 heaped teaspoon of organic, or active Manuka honey (expensive but the best)

What you do with it

Put the lot in your blender and blend until smooth—drink and enjoy!

Serves 1–2

The Melon Rouge

Can you can, can, can?
If not, try this ultimate system flusher—one for Ewan your friends!

You will need

 1 seeded watermelon—yep that's it!

What you do with it
Simply cut it into chunks and juice—including the skin. (Remember 95 percent of nutrients in a watermelon are to be found very close to and in the skin.)

The Desi and Juicy

A timeless pear, which you will rerun forever

You will need

- 🍓 A funny pear (make it 3 conference)
- 🍓 Bit of passion (well, he was a Latin—make that 1 passion fruit)
- 🍓 ½ a pineapple (from Cuba)
- 🍓 ¼ hilarious grapefruit (red)
- 🍓 4 ice cubes

What to do with it

Peel the pineapple and grapefruit and juice them together with the pears. Cut the top off the passion fruit, scoop out the inside, and place in a blender along with the juice and ice. Blend it all for 45 seconds and have a ball.

Strawberry Yields Forever

Well not quite forever, but they do yield a lot if you treat them right!

You will need

- 2 handfuls of fresh, ripe, gorgeous-smelling strawberries
- Handful of ice

What you do with it

Simply juice one handful of strawberries and pour into a blender along with the remaining handful of whole strawberries and the ice. Blend the lot. Once tasted, you really will want it to be forever. If you are in a hurry and don't want to use both machines, you can simply put all the strawberries into a blender with ice and a little water and blend.

Serves 1

The Jack "Sun" Five

**A little nutty, but makes your body move and makes you feel
soooooo good inside
It's easy as 1, 2, 3 do, ray, me!**

You will need

- 2 peaches
- Small glass of water
- Handful of ice
- Small handful of almond nuts
- Handful of frozen berries (your choice—Black Forest fruits are beautiful)
- ½ a pineapple
- 4 oranges
- ¼ grapefruit

What you do with it

Put the peaches in the blender (yes, take out the seed or you will
have no blender left!) add water, ice, nuts, and berries. Juice the
pineapple, oranges, and grapefruit, pour onto the other ingredients
in the blender, blend until smooth and creamy, then drink and let
your cells sing.

Serves 2–4

The Nutty "Gorge" Bush Junior

A little nuttier than the older version, but still super-powerful against internal foreign invaders

You will need

- 1 small handful of almond nuts
- 1 "big apple"
- 1 "Florida" orange
- 1 passion fruit
- ½ a lemon
- ½ a pineapple
- 1 banana
- Handful of ice

What you do with it

Peel the lemon, pineapple, banana, and orange. Cut the top off the passion fruit, scoop out the contents, and place in a blender along with the banana, nuts, and ice. Juice the lemon, pineapple, and orange and pour into the blender. Blend the lot for one minute.

PLEASE NOTE: To get this presidential smoothie to act faster on your internal invaders—simply add oil—of the omega-6 kind (this essential oil can be found in all good health food stores)!

Serves up to 4 years—oops I mean 1–2 people

The "No" Fats Domino

Unlike the real thing this blueberry thrill is 99 percent fat free, but still a real smoothie

You will need

- ½ a medium pineapple
- Large handful of fresh or frozen blueberries
- Small handful of fresh or frozen raspberries
- Pinch of cinnamon
- ½ a banana
- Handful of ice

What you do with it

Juice the pineapple and pour into a blender with all the other ingredients. Blend for 45 seconds to produce a smoothie that is sure to thrill.

Serves 2 (or 1 if you're really hungry)

You've Been Mangoed

This is a real wake-you-up face slapper!

You will need

- 1 large mango
- ½ a banana
- 1 lime
- Large handful of ice

What you do with it

Remove the stone from the mango (as explained in A–Z fruit and veg). Chop mango and place in a blender along with ½ a banana. Cut the lime in half and peel one half. Add this half to the blender along with the ice. Squeeze out the juice from the other half into the blender. Blend everything for 45 seconds until smooth.

Serves 1

Spring Break-Fast

.

**This super juice has a real touch of spring about it and is the
perfect way to break your fast**

You will need

- 4 oranges
- ¼ a pink grapefruit
- Spring water with bubbles (I recommend Perrier)
- 5 ice cubes

What you do with it

Juice the oranges and grapefruit. Pour into a blender, add a glass of
spring water, and the ice. Blend, pour, drink, and let the joys of
spring furnish every cell in your body.

Serves 1–2

The Congressman

Good for relaxing, when one needs to lie . . . down!

You will need (lots of pork and junket food, sorry I mean . . .)

- 🍓 1 handful of blackberries (so it "looks like America")
- 🍓 1 passion fruit (in the closet, preferably)
- 🍓 1 mango
- 🍓 1 kiwi
- 🍓 1 medium pineapple
- 🍓 1 handful of ice

What you need to do

Peel the mango, pineapple, and kiwi. Cut the top off the passion fruit, scoop out the contents, and place in a blender along with the blackberries, kiwi, and chopped mango. Juice the pineapple and pour into the blender. Blend it together and enjoy the goodness of a Congressman, but drink it fast before it goes bad.

Serves 2 years unless arrested, sorry I mean 1–2 people

A Real Peach

This is simply one of the easiest yet finest-tasting smoothies you can make

You will need
- 6 peaches
- Handful of ice

What you do with it

Remove the stones from the peaches and juice four of them. Pour into a blender with the ice and the remaining two peaches. Blend for 30 seconds, pour, and enjoy.

Serves 1

Time to Veg Out

The Juice Master Complete

Everything you will ever need in one juice—complete from A–Zinc!

This really is the ultimate in vegetable juices, or to be more accurate, vegetable smoothies, and I *highly* recommend one of these babies whenever you get the chance. All juices should be treated as a meal, or part of a meal, but this really *is* a meal. If you want a drink that's complete from A to zinc—look no further than The Juice Master Complete.

You will need

- ½ a lemon
- ½ a lime
- ¼ small pineapple
- 4 apples
- 8 carrots
- 2 large handfuls spinach
- 1 small raw beet
- ½ a cucumber
- 2 sticks celery
- Small head of broccoli
- ½ a pepper (any color)
- Piece of fennel about 2-inch square
- 1 bunch of parsley
- 1 bunch of watercress
- ¼-inch cube of ginger
- 1 small ripe avocado
- 1 half teaspoon of Udo's oil (optional)
- 1 heaped teaspoon of "live" acidophilus powder (optional)
- 1 teaspoon of lecithin granules
- 1 teaspoon of wheatgerm powder (optional)

What you do with it

Peel the ½ lemon, lime, and pineapple (unless organic, if so just wash and juice as they are). Juice three of the four apples, all the carrots, spinach, beet, cucumber, celery, broccoli, pepper, fennel, lemon, lime, pineapple, parsley, watercress, and ginger. Open the avocado and take out the stone. Scoop out the contents with a spoon, getting as close to the skin as possible. Chop up the remaining apple and place in the blender along with the avocado, juice, oil, acidophilus, lecithin granules, and wheatgerm powder. Blend at a low speed for just 30 seconds.

You can get Udo's essential oils, acidophilus, lecithin granules, and wheatgerm powder from any good health store. (Acidophilus is a friendly bacteria, excellent for all, but especially those who have candida, athlete's foot, thrush, etc.)

Serves 2–3

The Hawny Juice

Of the golden kind!

No—it doesn't make you feel horny. It is named after the beautiful Goldie Hawn. This juice is said to be one of the reasons behind why she stays looking so damn good. She is a huge juicing fan, and this is one of her daily faves.

You will need (the three Cs)

- 4 large carrots
- ½ a cucumber
- 3 sticks of celery

What you do with it

Juice the lot, stir, and enjoy the liquid goldie.

NOTE: This juice contains bio-blah-blah-noids, beta-whatsit, and vitamins blah and blah. As I will repeat, WE DON'T NEED TO KNOW! As long as we have it coming into our bodies, it doesn't matter what we call them. All the fruit and veggie juices have bundles of live nutrition which benefit ALL areas of the body. So just juice and go.

The Anne Robin"sun"

Cool as a cucumber with a little ginger on top!
Who's lost their minerals?
Who can't stand the heat in the kitchen?
Who's lost their way on the road to health?
Who doesn't know a carrot from a turnip?

It's time to juice up . . . The Strongest Zinc

You will need (a strong nerve, sorry I mean . . .)

- 6 carrots
- 3 apples
- ¼ cucumber
- 1 stick of celery
- Bit of ginger
- 4 Brazil nuts
- Small palmful of sunflower seeds
- Small palmful of pumpkin seeds

What you do with it

Be as rude as possible to everyone around you . . . no, I mean juice the carrots, apples, cucumber, celery, and ginger and pour into a blender. Add nuts and seeds and blend for a while to make sure all have been liquefied—pour and enjoy.

They say you are what you eat, in that case after this little beauty, you are the strongest zinc—GOODBYE!

JM TIP: Brazil nuts, sunflower, and pumpkin seeds are all naturally high in zinc, which is particularly good for skin disorders.

Serves 2

The Crisp Rock

**Very sharp, with a chiseled edge, not too heavy, and
has the ability to make you smile!**

You will need

- 1 lime
- 1 inch piece of ginger
- 4 large carrots
- 2 Royal Gala apples
- ¼ cucumber

What you do with it

Cut the veg and fruits to size of chute and juice the lot. Leave the
skin on the lime—it's what makes the Rock so sharp.

Serves 1

The Anthony Robbins

**Not as effective as the real thing for stimulating
the mind, but it's close!
This is an absolute giant of a juice designed to feed your
six human needs: protein, carbohydrate, fats, water, vitamins,
and minerals**

All the fruit and veg juices in this book contain the above six in various degrees, but like the Juice Master Complete, this is designed to give you your daily dose in one complete juice.

You will need

- ¼ pineapple
- ½ a lemon
- 5 carrots
- 3 apples
- ½ a yellow pepper
- 1 stick celery
- 1 spear asparagus
- ¼-inch piece of ginger
- 1 handful of wheatgrass (only include if you have a masticating juicer)
- 1 large handful of spinach
- 1 bunch watercress
- 1 bunch parsley
- ½ an avocado
- Handful of ice
- 1 teaspoon of kelp powder (optional)
- 1 teaspoon of "live" acidophilus (optional)

What you do with it

Peel ¼ pineapple and ½ lemon (unless organic) and juice along with everything except the last 4 ingredients. Scoop out the avocado from its skin and place in blender. Add ice, kelp powder, acidophilus, and the juice. Blend for 20 seconds then serve.

Serves 2–3

NOTE: Kelp powder and acidophilus are optional and can be found in any good health food store. Acidophilus helps to replace friendly bacteria in your gut.

The Minty Hawn

This, like The Hawney Juice, is named after Goldie herself. She's a big juicing fan and seemingly worth a mint—so why not!

You will need

- 6 carrots
- 1 celery stick
- ⅓ cucumber
- Small handful of fresh mint

What you do with it

Simply juice the carrots, celery, and cucumber, then finely chop the mint and stir into the juice.

Serves 1–2

The Hoover

Gives you a lift!
Picks up rubbish from your blood, cleans out your colon,
and all without the need for a bag!

You will need

- Apple and carrot base—as much as you like
- 1 palm-sized raw beet
- 2 sticks of celery
- ½ a medium cucumber
- Good handful of spinach

What you do with it

Juice the lot, stir, pour, and enjoy.

Serves as many as you like.

The Iron Lady

No 'tis not a Mrs. Thatcher. We're talking real iron here and this one's full of it!

You will need

- Some carrots and apples (crapple base)—enough to make 50–75 percent of the overall content of juice
- Piece of broccoli
- Handful of spinach
- Handful of kale (if juicing with a centrifugal machine, add more spinach and leave out the kale—this tends to juice well only with a Green Life juicer)

What you do with it

Juice the lot, pour, and enjoy.

NOTE: You can use organically grown green stuff, but unless you own something like a Green Life juicer, there is a lot of waste. I do, however, tend to use organic carrots and apples for the base even if I'm using my centrifugal juicer.

The Iron Mike Ty"sun"

Packs a punch and plenty of bite!

You will need

- 2 very large handfuls of spinach
- ½ a medium pineapple
- 6 carrots
- 2 apples
- Very small piece of ginger

What you do with it
Round 1: Juice the lot.

Round 2: Unusual for it to go beyond Round 1 with Mr. Ty"Sun" as it's usually down in one, but I don't advise this, so please drink slowly.

Serves 1–2

NOTE: Remember, most of the quantities I give are for about a pint of juice; always adjust accordingly depending on how many people and how hungry you are. Always bear in mind the drinks are small meals in themselves.

Chive Alive

A different sort of orange juice

You will need

🍓 6 carrots
🍓 Small handful of fresh organic chives

What you do with it
Juice the carrots and finely chop the chives. Add the chives to the juice, stir, and enjoy.

The Six-Carrot Diamond

A gem of a concoction

You will need

- 6 carrots
- 1 apple
- 1 stick of celery
- 1-inch piece of ginger
- ¼ pineapple
- ½ a lime with skin on

What you do with it

Simply cut all the ingredients to the size of chute and juice the lot.

Serves 1–2

The Thrill Clinton

"I did not have 'juicy' relations with that girl"
An easy one to swallow—and there's no comeback!

You will need (an understanding partner, more bull than a rodeo show, the unique ability to smoke a joint without inhaling, sorry I mean . . .)

- 4 carrots
- 2 apples
- 4 medium radishes
- ½ a lime (peeled)
- Handful of parsley

What you do with it
Juice the lot, pour, and enjoy.

Serves 1

The Broccoli Spears

Oh baby, baby—a juice *virgin* on the divine—or so we thought!

You will need

- "Crapple" base (apple and carrot)
- 2 big handfuls of broccoli (including spears)
- ¼ large cucumber (for that clean, fresh-faced look)

What you do with it

Simply juice the lot and let your system feel "Stronger" (that's a Britney song in case you didn't know) while your cells are singing "Hit me baby one more time."

As with all juices/smoothies, adjust the quantities depending on the amount of juice required.

Ginger Rogers and Fred A. Pear

A truly unbelievable combination

You will need

- ½ a lemon
- 2 tomatoes
- 5 carrots
- ¼ inch piece of ginger
- 3 apples
- ½ a ripe avocado

What you do with it

Juice the lemon, tomatoes, carrots, apples, and ginger. Put the avocado pear in a blender, then add the juice. Blend until creamy and let the nutrients dance with your cells.

Serves 2

The Enron

Designed to totally clean you out! Perhaps this is the only time it's worth investing in an "Enron"—this one actually helps to replenish your bank account (of the enzyme kind at least)!

You will need

- 10 carrots
- 1 raw beetroot
- ½ a cucumber
- 1 stick of celery
- 2 large handfuls of spinach
- 1 handful of broccoli
- ¼ lime
- ¼ lemon

What you do with it

Top and tail the carrots and peel the lemon and lime. Juice everything and if warm, place in a blender with a little ice. Pour, drink, and know that every time you have an "Enron" you have added to your net worth of pure life force.

Serves 2–3

A Gala Affair

Will put you in a festive mood!

You will need

- 6 apples (Gala)
- ½ a lime (peeled)
- 1 small beet
- 1 bunch of parsley
- 1 handful of spinach
- 3 radishes

What you do with it

Juice the lot, pour, and drink slowly.

Serves 1–2

The Michael Jordan

**A powerful juice that's a slam dunk against illnesses and
makes your skin glow!**

You will need

- 5 apples
- Handful of spinach
- ½ a lime (peeled)
- ½ a cucumber
- ½ a yellow pepper
- ½ an orange pepper
- 1 teaspoon of acidophilus
- Pinch of nutmeg powder

What you do with it

Juice the apples, spinach, lime, cucumber, and yellow and orange
peppers. Add the acidophilus and nutmeg powder, stir, and unlike
the real Michael, please try not to dribble!

Serves 1–2

The Steven "Meal"burg

Get your *jaws* into this one — its *duel* action will help to *E.T.* (eliminate toxins)

This is more of a meal than a juice as it contains a few "whole" fruit and veggies.

Who's in this one?

- 4 carrots
- 2 apples
- 1 bunch of parsley
- 2 radishes
- ½ a lemon (peeled)
- Handful of dandelion greens (or use spinach)
- ½ a cucumber
- ½-inch piece of ginger
- ½ an avocado
- Pinch of cinnamon powder

Here's your direction
Juice the carrots, *one* of the apples, parsley, radishes, lemon, dandelion greens (or spinach), ¼ of the cucumber and ginger. Scoop out the flesh from the avocado and place in a blender. Cut the remaining apple and cucumber into small pieces and add to the blender, add the juice, blend for 60 seconds, and serve. Remember to drink slowly and "chew" your juice.

Serves 1–2

Turnip, Turnip, Turnip

**There's a vegetable for every purpose
under heaven.**

You will need

- 1 turnip (not 3)
- 1 handful of dandelion greens
- 4 carrots

What you do with it

Juice the lot. This isn't the best-tasting juice in the world but to everything there is a season—and it's great for your bones.

Serves 1

Nip in the Bod

Parsnips, that is — not as bad as it sounds.

You will need

- 4 carrots
- 2 apples (Royal Gala if possible)
- Small handful of mint leaves
- Small handful of spinach
- ½-inch piece of ginger
- ¼ a parsnip
- ½ a lime

What you do with it

Juice the lot, remembering to push mint, ginger, and spinach through the juicer in between the apples. Pour and enjoy.

Serves 1 (generously)

Brad Pip and Jennifer Aniseed

Invite your friends round for a taste of this beautiful juice

You will need

- 6 carrots
- 1 palm-sized bulb of fennel
- ½-inch piece ginger
- 1 handful of parsley
- ¼ cucumber
- 1 stick of celery
- 1 handful of dandelion greens (use spinach if these are unavailable)

What you do with it

Juice the lot, pour, and enjoy this aniseed-flavored beauty. Although it's excellent for your weight, bones, and skin, it may not have the ability to turn you into Brad or Jenny, but hey—even nature's miracles have their limits!

Serves 1–2

The Blockbuster

Starring

🍓 Avocado as Essential Fatty Acid (half)
🍓 King Carrot as Cancer Blaster (6)
🍓 Apples as Disease Crusher Granny Smith (4)
🍓 Mr. Tom ato as Vitamin C and E (3)
🍓 Broccoli as Iron Man (small handful)

Supporting

🍓 Lemon and Lime as two tasty geezers (½ lemon, 1 lime)
🍓 Green and Red chillies as Hot Stuff (half of each)

Action!

Scoop out the avocado flesh with a spoon. Juice the carrots, apples, tomatoes, broccoli, lemon, and lime. Cut the chillies into very fine pieces and put into a blender (add a couple of the hot seeds if you are brave!) with the avocado and juice. Blend until smooth.

Serves 2

"Thank you, it's been . . . emotional!"

THE END

Night-Time Juices

The Tom Snooze

A short, worth a mint!
Mission good night's sleep very possible

You will need

- 4 medium-sized tomatoes
- 3 apples
- 1 lime
- Some mint leaves
- Small piece of ginger

What you do with it

Juice the tomatoes, apples, and lime and chop the mint and ginger. Place everything in a pan and gently, in fact *very* gently, heat until warm, stirring occasionally

DO NOT BOIL, AS YOU WILL LOSE LIVE NUTRIENTS!

This drink should be taken warm about an hour before going to bed.

Try not to lose the ginger as it may cost you dearly in a divorce settlement!

Serves 1

The Marilyn Monroe

Some like it hot!

You will need

🍓 A good pear (I know, but come what did you expect?) — actually make it 2
🍓 4 apples
🍓 Large pinch of cinnamon

What you do with it
Juice the pears and apples and pour into a pan. Add a good sprinkling of cinnamon and heat very slowly and gently. Once again—

DO NOT BOIL THE NUTRIENTS TO DEATH!
(sorry for the outburst but 'tis important)

Pour this little beauty into a mug, add another sprinkle of cinnamon, and if you like you can always take your Marilyn Monroe to bed for a satisfying night's sleep.

Remember:
"A juice on the lips may be . . . quite con-tin-en-tal,
But diamonds are a girl's best friend"

Serves 1

The Freddy Kruger

A night pear on Elm Street

You will need

🍓 8 conference pears
🍓 Large pinch of cinnamon
🍓 ½-inch piece of ginger

What you do with it

Juice the pears and ginger then add them to a pan along with the cinnamon. Heat very slowly and gently—DO *NOT BOIL* THE NUTRIENTS TO DEATH (had to say it again, it's very important). Once nice and warm, pour out, sprinkle a little more cinnamon on top, and drink slowly. Sweet dreams—this is perhaps the only time a Freddy Kruger will actually help you to a peaceful night's sleep.

Serves 1

Nut-Meg Ryan

Sleepy in zzZZ apple!
Another good one to go to bed with!

You will need

- 3 apples
- Good pinch of cinnamon
- Good pinch of nutmeg
- 6 blackberries

What you do with it

Juice the apples and pour into blender with the other ingredients. Blend the lot and pour into a pan. Heat *slowly*, then pour into a mug and get snug as a bug in a rug for this Nut-Meg Ryan is designed to help you sleep like a baby—night, night X.

Serves 1

Glad-it's-Night and the Pips

Night time drink with strawberries

You will need

- 2 apples
- 2 conference pears
- 6 fresh strawberries

What you do with it

Juice the apples and pears and pour into a pan. Cut each strawberry into very small pieces and place in the pan. *Very gently* heat the contents, stirring constantly, and remembering not to boil the mixture. Pour into mug, get cosy, and after a hard day, you'll be glad it's night—sweet dreams.

Serves 1

Power Smoothies

All juices and smoothies are incredibly powerful, but for all you weight trainers and very active puppies out there, here's a couple of JM's muscle and energy builders.

Banana-Rama

A-me-know why it's essential
(That's essential amino acids in case it passed you by)

This is great for when you need some energy for running, weight training, working out, and so on.

You will need

- 3 bananas
- Small handful of almonds
- 1 cup of live organic goat's yogurt (if you're vegan just use small cup of soya milk and add a teaspoon of live acidophilus)
- Large handful of fresh or frozen blueberries
- Large handful of ice
- Small glass of mineral water (if using soy milk instead of yogurt, leave out the water)

What you do with It

This is such a quick and easy smoothie—there's no need for your juicer here, just your blender. Simply put all ingredients in blender and blend for 45 seconds to 1 minute (or until nuts have been chopped enough).

JM Fact—Amino acids are the building blocks for protein. We need 23 in all, luckily we already have 15, but the other 8 are what are known as essential amino acids—without them we would soon perish, so pretty essential then! The good news is that just one banana has many of the essential amino acids we need and that's before we've even started on the nuts!

Serves 1

The Hulk Hogain

An old blend but still as big and powerful as ever

This choc-tastic power smoothy is specially designed for all you budding wrestlers and body builders out there or those just looking to pack on a few more pounds.

You will need

- ½ a pineapple
- 4 oranges
- ½ a lime (peeled)
- Handful of grapes (any color, seeded or not)
- 2 bananas
- 1 cup of live organic goat's yogurt (if you're vegan just use a small cup of unsweetened organic soy milk and add teaspoon full of live acidophilus)
- 1 heaped tablespoon of soy protein powder
- 1 teaspoon of Manuka active honey (if unavailable, use organic or whatever you have)
- 1 teaspoon of carob powder (if you hate the taste of chocolate skip this)

What you do with it

Peel the pineapple (unless it's organic) and oranges, remembering to keep as much of the white pith on the oranges as possible. Juice ½ a pineapple, lime, grapes, and oranges and pour into blender. Add the bananas, yogurt, protein powder, honey, and carob powder and blend.

Serves 1–2

Dr. Juice!

Make no mistake, all juices have therapeutic values—but some have more of a bite than others. The following two juices are designed to help you through your ills.

The Schwarzenegger

The original germinator

You won't win any friends with this, but it's a must when viruses pounce! This is also good for helping to keep the arteries open and contains the amazing blood cleanser—beet.

You will need

- 1 garlic clove
- 2 apples
- 1-inch piece of ginger
- 4 carrots
- 2 spears of asparagus
- Handful of parsley
- 1 raw beetroot
- Stick of celery
- ½ a cucumber
- 1 teaspoon of wheatgerm powder (for added fiber)
- 1 teaspoon of acidophilus (helps replace friendly bacteria)

What you do with it

Juice the lot and simply stir in the wheatgerm and acidophilus. When juicing garlic, cut a hole in a section of apple and push in the garlic. The idea is to make sure the garlic doesn't directly touch the machine, you really don't want everything tasting of garlic from here on in.

Serves 1 poorly person

The "Phil" Good Collins

**When I'm feeling blue, all I have to do . . . is make a juice for you—
oh I mean me!**

You will need

- 2 garlic cloves
- 1-inch piece of ginger
- ½ a small red onion
- 6 carrots
- 1 beet
- ½ a pineapple
- 4 radishes
- 1 handful of parsley
- ½ a cucumber
- 1 teaspoon of Udo's oil
- 1 teaspoon of acidophilus powder
- 1 teaspoon of wheatgerm powder

What you do with it

Juice everything and then add oil, acidophilus, and wheatgerm.
Remember to take the skin off the pineapple if it's not organic and make
sure to push the garlic gloves into the pineapple flesh to avoid contact
with the machine.

Serves 1 sick puppy

Keeping It Cool!

These super-cool natural ice creams are just fab for kids and adults alike.
They taste like ice cream, but without all the cow glue and white refined
sugar! *Some* of the following require a masticating juice extractor. They
have a homogenizer slide, making it possible to turn frozen fruits into
instant ice cream!

The Hanni"ball"

A bit of a chiller—a real I scream!

You will need

- 3 small cone-shaped plastic cups (used for making frozen treats)
- 3 frozen "skinless" bananas
- Handful of frozen black/blueberries
- 1 small cup of live organic goats yogurt or ½ cup of organic unsweetened soy milk
- Pinch of cinnamon powder
- 3 black grapes

What you do with it

Simply put frozen bananas, berries, and yogurt or soy milk in a blender and add a pinch of cinnamon. Blend until thick and creamy. Put one black grape in the base of each plastic cone and pour the mixture on top. Drink as is or eat with a spoon.

Serves 3

The John Travolta

Super cool

You will need

- 1 masticating juice extractor (sorry to all those with only a centrifugal!)
- Handful of frozen raspberries
- 1 frozen peeled kiwi
- ½ a frozen peeled lemon
- 1 banana
- Pinch of cinnamon powder

What you do with it

Prefreeze fruits in plastic container, always remembering to peel and chop first. Place "homogenizer" slide on your machine, then simply push through ingredients. Place natural ice cream in bowl, add cinnamon and enjoy.

Serves 1

Fourth of July

A touch of red, white, and blue

You will need

- 🍓 1 cool Royal Gala apple
- 🍓 1 frozen kiwi fruit
- 🍓 Handful of frozen blueberries
- 🍓 Handful of frozen red berries
- 🍓 1 frozen banana
- 🍓 1 cup of organic unsweetened soy milk

What you do with it

Place all the ingredients in a blender. Blend until thick and creamy. Enjoy the fireworks!

Serves 1–2

The Titanic

This icy beauty goes down well

You will need

- 1 cool pineapple
- ½ a frozen peeled lime
- 1 de-stoned frozen peach
- 1 passion fruit
- ½ cup of organic live goats yogurt or unsweetened organic soy milk if vegan
- ½ cup of frozen blackberries

What you do with it

Juice pineapple and pour into a blender along with all the other ingredients. Blend until creamy—simply beautiful!

Serves 2–3

Vanilla Ice, Ice Baby

An icy one-hit wonder!

You will need

- 1 masticating juice extractor
- 2 frozen bananas
- ¼ frozen peeled lemon
- ¼ frozen peeled pineapple
- Handful of berries (your choice)
- 4 frozen mint leaves
- Pinch of vanilla seeds

What you do with it

Prefreeze the fruits in a plastic container, always remembering to peel and chop first. Place "homogenizer" slide on your machine, then simply push through ingredients. Place natural ice cream in bowl, sprinkle with vanilla seeds, and enjoy! (If you don't have a vanilla bean, add a drop of vanilla extract.)

Serves 1–2

Super-Fast Smoothies

For when you just have to up and go.

The following smoothies are for when you need super-fast nutrition in super-fast time—no need for a juicer here!

The Mike-Cool Andretti

Still super cool and super fast!

You will need

- 1 cup of organic live goat's yogurt or 1 cup of unsweetened organic soy milk with a spoonful of acidophilus powder
- 1 handful of blackberries (fresh or frozen)
- 1 banana
- 4 cubes ice
- 6 almonds

What you do with it

Put the lot into a blender. Blend for 45 seconds for a super-cool glass of live nutrition designed to fuel your amazing vehicle in the fastest possible way.

Serves 1–2

The Carl Lewis

One hell of a super-fast smoothie. Add this one to your lunch-box!

On your marks—shop for the following

- 2 seeded plums (oh stop it!)
- 1 large banana (now you're getting silly)
- Handful of strawberries
- 2 peeled kiwi fruits
- Glass of soy milk
- Handful of ice
- Pinch of cinnamon powder

Get set—get your blender ready
Go—put the lot into a blender. Blend for 9.96 seconds (actually better blend for 45 seconds to be sure), pour into cool glass and enjoy.

Serves 1–2

The Juice Master's Wholefood Recipes

I know this is a primarily a juice/smoothie book, but many of you will want to go on the Ultimate Spring Cleaning Plan and have your weekly natural day. With that in mind, here are just a couple of snack and salad ideas for you to get your teeth into.

The Juice Master's Natural Salad

This meal is just perfect for your weekly "natural" day and excellent for The Juice Master's Ultimate Spring Cleaning Plan.

You will need

- ½ bag of young leaf spinach
- ½ bag of rocket
- ½ bag of watercress
- 1 red onion
- ½ a red pepper
- ½ an orange pepper
- ½ a yellow pepper
- ⅓ medium cucumber

- 1 carrot
- Small handful of red cabbage
- Small handful of white cabbage
- Handful of alfalfa sprouts
- 2 large ripe avocados
- 1 lemon
- 1 lime
- 8 cherry tomatoes

What you do with it

Tear the baby leaf spinach into small pieces and place in a large salad bowl along with the rocket leaves and watercress. Chop the red onion, peppers, and cucumber into small pieces and add to the bowl. Grate the carrot and white and red cabbages and sprinkle into the bowl along with the alfalfa sprouts. Cut the avocados in half and take out the seed (if ripe the seed should come out easily). Scoop out the creamy flesh, cut into pieces, and add to the bowl. Cut the lemon and lime in half, squeeze onto the salad, add the tomatoes, and toss it all together.

Serves 2–3

JM's Snack Attack

**When hunger hits and you sense an apple just ain't gonna cut it—
try this little beauty**

It has to be my absolute favorite snack, and it's just soooo good for you. This recipe is suitable for a lunchtime meal on the Juice Master's Spring Cleaning Plan, but only after day seven.

You will need

- 2 slices of rye bread
- 1 ripe avocado
- 3.75oz can boneless sardines in oil
- 1 lemon

What you do with it

Toast the rye bread. Cut open the avocado, take out the seed, and scoop out the creamy flesh. Spread the avocado on the toasted bread. Open the sardines, drain off the excess oil, and put equal amounts on each slice of avocado-spread rye toast. Cut the lemon in half and squeeze liquid over it. Eat slowly, savor the flavors, and enjoy!

Serves 1—maybe 2 if you're feeling generous!

JM's Tuna, Avocado, Spinach, and Mayo Salad

So quick, so easy, and soooo filling

This salad can also be used as part of the spring-cleaning plan, but again only after day seven.

You will need

- ½ bag of baby leaf spinach
- 1 can tuna (in water, oil, or brine—whatever you like)
- 1 tablespoon of organic mayonnaise (yes, mayonnaise)
- 1 large ripe avocado
- 1 lemon

What you do with it

Tear the spinach leaves into small pieces and place on a large plate. Open the tuna and place in a small bowl. Add the mayo and mix. Open the avocado and remove the seed. Scoop out the flesh. Slice the avocado into strips and place on the bed of spinach along with the tuna mayo. Cut the lemon in half and squeeze over the lot. Eat slowly, savor the flavors and enjoy!

Serves 1—perhaps 2 at a push

JM's Pasta and Pesto

(with veggie juice starter)

As mentioned, I'm not a 100 percent raw-fooder and at the moment have no intentions of becoming one. What I teach is nutrition for reality, and in the real world we all like some cooked food. The idea is to make it as healthy as possible.

You will need

- 5 ounces of hemp and spelt pasta (if you cannot get hold of this please use wholegrain)
- 1 small bottle of green pesto
- 4 carrots
- Large handful of spinach
- ½ a lime
- Large handful of parsley

What you do with it

Fill a pan with water and place on heat. While it's heating up, juice the carrots, spinach, lime, and parsley. Place the pasta in the boiling water for the time specified on the packet (usually 8 minutes). Drink the juice as a starter while you're waiting for the pasta. Drain the pasta and place into a largish bowl. Open the pesto and mix it into the pasta. Eat slowly and enjoy!

You can, of course, make your own pesto, but as this is a fast-food book I'm suggesting quick and easy meals.

Serves 1

JM's Guacamole

Av-o-look at this beauty!

This is my favorite dip by far—and it's not only scrumptious, it's good for you.

You will need

- 6 medium ripe avocados
- Juice of 2 lemons
- 1 garlic clove
- 2 tomatoes
- 1 red or white onion
- Handful of chives
- 2 small green chillies (optional—if you do use them, leave out the seeds)

What you do with it

Put the avocados into a blender (peel and seed them first) and add lemon juice. Put the garlic through a garlic press and add to the blender. Make sure you push the avocado well into the blender with a spoon. Blend the ingredients until creamy (you may have to stop and start the blender a few times and keep moving the ingredients around). Finely chop the tomatoes, onion, chives, and chillies. Spoon out the creamy avocado dip from the blender and place it in a bowl. Add the remaining ingredients and mix together. Serve with just about anything and enjoy!

JM's Almond and Banana Milk

This is a great alternative to cow's milk and is excellent poured on some jumbo oats; dried and whole fruits; and whole, natural nuts to make a scrumptious, healthy muesli.

You will need

- Handful of almonds
- 1 banana
- 1 large cup of water
- Small handful of ice

What you do with it
Place all the ingredients in a blender. Blend for 1 minute or until all the nuts have blended in and serve. If it's too thick, add more water.

16
Questions and Answers

Should I wash or peel produce before juicing?
Wash yes, peel no. Most of the nutrients are found just beneath the skin, so keep the skin on where possible. The exceptions are bananas, grapefruits; oranges; and nonorganic lemons, limes, and pineapples. When in doubt, check out the A–Z of fruit and veg for guidance on individual produce.

Should I always use organic produce?
Where possible buy "organic"—it is better, but don't lose sleep if you can't afford it or get hold of it; the other stuff is still loaded with oodles of goodness. As long as you wash your produce, all fruits and veg can only do you good. Also, when you juice, most of the outer layer ends up in the pulp anyway.

What's the difference between a smoothie and a juice?
A smoothie is a combination of *whole* soft fruits and either milk, yogurt, ice, or fruit juice mixed together in a blender. The only milk you will find in my smoothies is soy milk and the only yogurt I use is live, organic goat's yogurt. On the whole I tend to use fruit juice and ice. The reason for adding juice is so that the mixture isn't too thick. This is the biggest mistake people make when making smoothies—

they tend to just stick whole fruits into a blender and whisk them up. If you do this it always tends to be far too thick, so add liquid or a very large handful of ice. You can deliberately make it thick and eat it like an ice cream (for an example see The Hanni"ball" on page 231).

Does freezing fruit kill it like cooking?
No it doesn't. When you freeze raw produce for a short space of time you only lose about 5 percent of the enzymes.

I've already got a blender and food processor, do I still need to buy a juicer?
Yes. A food processor or blender only chops the "whole" foods, a juicer extracts the juice from the fibers.

You don't mention salad or lettuce—if it's looking a bit sad to eat, can I juice my salad with other things?
Yep, although I really wouldn't bother with stuff like iceberg lettuce, as it's not exactly tops on the nutrition front.

There seems like a lot of waste, can I use the pulp for anything?
The best place for it is on your garden; it makes wonderful compost. You can use it for soups and such, but it's better to use whole veg and some juice.

The juice is a little frothy and sometimes there's clear liquid at the bottom and thick frothy stuff at the top—is this normal?
Yes. Many juices "separate" quite quickly. When this happens simply stir and drink; do not scoop out the thick, frothy stuff—it contains heaps of nutrients.

I see in the recipes you use some herbs and spices, can I add different ones?
Most definitely, there are many herbs and spices you can add to your juices to give them a little oomph. Do be careful however, as herbs are pretty potent; never have just "herb juice"—always mix with the juice

of vegetables or fruit. You can add just about any herb you like—mint, rosemary, whatever, and all kinds of different spices really do add, well, some spice! If you like the taste of chocolate but don't want the caffeine and sugar that go along with it, get hold of some carob powder and add to some fruit smoothies—kids just love it.

What about dried fruits—can I add these to smoothies?

Yes you can, but whatever you do please don't try to juice them! Be careful with dried fruit, as it is high in concentrated fruit sugars, so use sparingly or not at all if diabetic. I do use them at times, as they are just so delicious, especially figs. If you want to add a few raisins, dates, apricots, figs, prunes, and so on, to your smoothies, feel free.

You don't list many common fruits and veg, like zucchini for example. Is there a reason for this and can I juice all fruits and veg?

The reason I haven't listed all fruits and veg is mainly due to the fact there are thousands of different types and this book would have been the size of the Napa valley had I included them all. I have included the ones that you will use the most and those that will do you most good. You can juice just about any fruit or veg (the exceptions being banana and avocado), and please feel free to do so. You will notice that I've included some veg in the recipes that I don't list in the A–Z of fruit and veg, like onion, for example. The reason is you will only use things like onion juice once in a blue moon, and you are much more likely and much better off eating them. If you want to try a fruit or veg I haven't listed—go ahead. Just remember that many need to be mixed with other sweeter juices, like apple and carrot.

What juices do you recommend I have with meals?

Vegetable juices—preferably ones without any apple (just add more carrot). Sip them with a meal or have one as a starter. I don't suggest having fruit juices or smoothies with a cooked food meal. You can also have a veg juice fifteen minutes before eating; you'll find you then need less of the main course (excellent if you want to lose weight).

You mention that cow's milk wasn't meant for humans, so why then do you add goat's yogurt to some smoothies?

Cow's milk is much harder for our systems to digest than goat's. Cow's milk was designed for a species with FOUR stomachs, we, like goats, have just the one. You will also notice that I only recommend "live" organic goat's yogurt. Live yogurt contains friendly bacteria that are necessary for good health. Again, if we'd been eating "live" foods all our lives then we would have plenty of healthy bacteria in our gut; as it is, most of us don't have enough, and getting a good dose of live friendly bacteria is a must. If you are vegan you can buy "live" acidophilus powder (found in many good health shops)—just make sure you get the stuff from the fridge.

Are there any shop-bought vegetable juices you recommend?

Unfortunately there isn't one on the market at the moment that I can recommend. I'm piloting The Juice Master Complete (which keeps its life-force intact for forty-eight to seventy-two hours) in shops in East Dulwich, where I live, so if all goes well, you could well see the *only* "live" freshly made vegetable smoothie in a shop near you very soon. As for fruit juices, again they are almost always enzyme "dead," but if you want a smoothie juice while you're out and about, go for the 100 percent pure fruit versions.

You give the impression that there are good foods and bad foods—but surely *all* foods are good to some extent, given that we would die without them?

I agree that there's no such thing as a bad food when there's no choice. Trust me, if I was unfortunate enough to ever find myself literally starving, I would eat whatever was available. In that situation, yes *all* foods are excellent—even sugar. But we *do* have a choice, and when you do there is such a thing as good and bad food. We are in the very fortunate position of being able to choose foods that will not just sustain life but protect against disease and improve our quality of life.

OK so what is the best food for humans above any other?

There's no such thing as one single best food, but there is a commonality in foods meant for human consumption. The four things *all* food ideally meant for human consumption have in common are:

1. They are unprocessed (you won't find a cooker in nature that's for sure!)
2. They contain "live," easily utilized nutrients and oodles of enzymes
3. They have been predigested by the plant (so require little or no energy to break down, assimilate, and eliminate)
4. *All*, without exception, are full of "pure liquid gold"

You mention the book *Slim 4 Life* quite a lot, is it just for overweight people?

NO, NO, NO, NO and in case you missed it—NO! Although the main title is *Slim 4 Life,* the subtitle is *Freedom from the Food Trap.* This was my first published book and went to number two on the bestsellers list in Ireland and continues to do very well in the UK. By word fo mouth alone, it has found its way to Australia, Dubai, France, Germany, India, Israel, New Zealand, Scandinavia, and many other places around the world. Many people, some who have never suffered from being overweight, have used the book to free themselves of their battle with food and health. The book is designed for anyone who eats food—which pretty much covers everyone. It is also designed to mentally free people from the food trap for life, no more dieting, no more restrictions, just healthy eating. I truly believe that everyone should read it, not simply because I wrote it, but because I know the potential impact it can have on your life. Here are just a couple of quotes from genuine, unsolicited letters:

"Wow—I'm half way through your amazing book for the second time. It's such an easy read … I'm getting it for a friend of mine as a birthday present. She's been on a diet for a while and while she has lost weight, she is always thinking about what she's missing out on. I've told her all about your book and she's really excited to read it!" **Cat**

"Quite simply brilliant!!" **Barbara**

"Hi Jason, THANKYOU, THANKYOU, THANKYOU for your brilliant book. I just cannot put it down. There is so much sense in what you are saying. After doing my own research into sugar and food addiction I have come to realize that this is my problem. This is the reason that as I have got older, even after trying to stick to a diet and breaking it after two weeks, time and time again, I am now at my heaviest weight ever. Not for long though!! Even my husband who is very much a "Eat as little fruit and veg as possible" kind of person, is reading the book and after just a few days of cutting out the rubbish is hooked on this new (or should we say "old") way of thinking and eating. Just as with 'The Good Book,' I believe that every home should have a copy of *Slim 4 Life*. Thanks again and you will no doubt hear from me again when I let you know how we've been getting on." **Lynne P**

"I'd just like to thank you for the most amazing book I've ever read in my life. I never would have believed that this collection of pages could be so interesting." **Ms Cooke**

… have lost half a stone, am juicing like mad, don't even want to reach for a chocolate bar!!! Peter has even refused a steak!!! You have had an astonishing effect on my life … and bowels" **Jo**

THE JUICE MASTER'S PAGE

For information on the Juice Master's videos, books, CDs, tapes, up-and-coming Slim 4 Life seminars, Stop Smoking seminars, Quit Alcohol program, private sessions—plus anything else you need to know

Call the Juice Master Hotline at **011 44 0845 1 30 28 29**

Address: 15 Soames Street, East Dulwich, London SE15 4BZ, England
Email: info@thejuicemaster.com   Website: www.thejuicemaster.com

For information on where to buy the juicing machines/blenders, mini-trampolines etc., mentioned in this book, please go to the main Website (www.thejuicemaster.com) or phone the Juice Master hotline. New machines are being developed all the time, so there is a possibility that the ones mentioned in this book are no longer the best on the market—always check the Website to see what's new.

If in the U.S., have a look for a Jamba Juice near you!

If you're in the fine city of Dublin and fancy a fresh juice while out and about please check out NUDE at one of the following addresses:

Nude
21 Suffolk Street
Dublin 2
Tel 6774804 Fax 6725773

Go Nude
103 Lr Lesson Street
Dublin 2
Tel 6615650

Nude
BT2
Grafton Street
Dublin 2
Tel 605666 ask for Nude

Nude
Georges Quay Plaza
Dublin 2
Tel 6774661 Fax 6774662